RECRUITING AND MANAGING VOLUNTEERS IN LIBRARIES

A How-To-Do-It Manual

BONNIE F. McCUNE
CHARLESZINE "TERRY" NELSON

*HOW-TO-DO-IT MANUALS
FOR LIBRARIANS*

Number 51

NEAL-SCHUMAN PUBLISHERS, INC.
New York, London

Published by Neal-Schuman Publishers, Inc.
100 Varick Street
New York, NY 10013

Printed and bound in the United States of America

Library of Congress Cataloging-in-Publication Data

McCune, Bonnie F.
    Recruiting and managing volunteers in libraries : a how-to-do-it
manual / by Bonnie F. McCune, Charleszine Nelson.
        p.   cm.
    Includes bibliographical references and index.
    ISBN 1-55570-204-X
    1. Volunteer workers in libraries—United States.   I. Nelson,
Charleszine.   II. Title.
Z682.4.V64M38   1995
021.7—dc20
                                                    95-4656
                                                    CIP

CONTENTS

                 How Do You Spell "Success"?
                 Analyzing Materials and Methods
                 The Final Evaluation

Chapter 7:   Community Service Volunteers   **103**
                 The Process

Chapter 8:   The R & R of Volunteerism—Reward and Recognition   **119**
                 Rewards from the Job
                 Formal Recognition
                 Special Event Volunteers
                 Informal Recognition
                 Staff Volunteers

Chapter 9:   Academic, School, and Special Libraries   **135**
                 The Budget and Planning Dilemma
                 Recruitment Techniques
                 Training
                 Reward and Recognition
                 The Importance of Planning and Evaluation
                 Turn Negatives into Positives
                 Utilize the Positives
                 Never Too Old To Learn

Chapter 10:   Troubleshooting   **145**

Chapter 11:   Types of Volunteer Programs   **157**

                 Appendix A   **169**

                 Index   **171**

PREFACE

The two authors of this book have had the equivalent of four careers in nonprofit groups that use volunteers. In addition to actual employment, we've served as volunteers of all types. We've organized cleaning crews, headed up garage sales, served on boards, and published newsletters and magazines. During our involvement we have experienced the panic of a financial shortfall and the euphoria of a successful poetry reading.

We believe in volunteerism and are keenly aware of its positive effects on a library. We know its strengths and its challenges. This handbook condenses our knowledge gained through years of experience and offers it to you in an informal and practical fashion. The book utilizes a broad-based approach, comprised of numerous parts with many essential details. We trust that every library will find useful ideas, regardless of the size of the institution or the development stage of its volunteer program.

Of course there are intangibles which cannot be taught. The critical elements of any volunteer effort are enthusiasm, flexibility, innovation, and humanity.

Basically, we feel the important thing for you to do is—begin. Don't get hung up on methodology or statistics. Management of volunteers is a learning process. Managers in volunteer administration must be social scientists and observers of human affairs. They use knowledge and techniques from other fields to do their jobs. As they learn, their programs and institutions progress.

We would like to thank the libraries that responded to our informal survey and sent sample materials and ideas. Special thanks go to Linda Fegley, Training Officer at the Denver Public Library; Jan Novak, District Media Resource Teacher, Aurora Public Schools; Jody Gehrig, Manager of Educational Resource Services, Denver Public Schools; Maria Blake, Indianapolis-Marion County Public Library; Julie Crowell, Judicial Services Program Manager, Arapahoe County Community Services Department; Catherine Childs, Volunteer Services Coordinator, Boulder Public Library; and Ryan Ellis, Community Service Specialist, Jefferson County Department of Corrections.

Bonnie F. McCune
Charleszine "Terry" Nelson
April, 1995

INTRODUCTION

Volunteers constructed the very foundation of our way of life. From the members of a Pilgrim congregation who shared food and clothing with the less fortunate, to the founding fathers striving with no financial recompense to create a government, people labored out of love, interest, or concern.

Down through the years, volunteers strengthened every endeavor in our society. Volunteerism is our legacy. Consider for a moment what we would lack without volunteers: Scouts, little league athletic teams, Sunday school, hospitality in health care facilities, community theater, most political endeavors, college alumni support, fund–raising events for the arts, human rights activism, and temporary families for exchange students to name a few.

To this list you can add library services. Volunteers in the libraries aren't new. Volunteers, in fact, organized libraries throughout the country as the wagon trains went west. Perhaps you recall a mom who helped in the summer by pasting stars on your vacation reading program certificate. Your memories encompass a grandfatherly guide on your first visit to the big downtown library.

What's changed are the conditions of our society. As libraries become more complex (just like business, government, finance, and every other arena), as technology booms and impacts all aspects of our lives, volunteerism has responded. Yes, there's still room for heartfelt commitment and love of books. But to respond to the needs of libraries as institutions and their patrons as customers, staff must use the same management skills applied to employees and project administration.

We can't afford the time or money to depend upon chance to attract and train volunteers. We don't have the energy to spare to remedy the chaos left in the wake of a well-intentioned but inept individual.

Libraries must view management of volunteers as deserving the same professionalism as collection development, reference, budgeting, and children's services. If we want, indeed *require,* people as committed to their volunteer duties as salaried employees, we must uphold our side of the contract, whether it's written or simply understood. We must recruit, train, retain, and supervise volunteers in the most effective manner possible.

This handbook provides an overview of every aspect of volunteerism for libraries. We begin with the theoretical — assessing your current status, developing goals and objectives, considering official policies and legal concerns. Then we immediately plunge into practicalities of everyday activities. How do you get volunteers in the first place, and furthermore, the right ones for a particular job?

Once you have the volunteers, who manages them and in what fashion? Major sections of the book help you develop your own (and other staff members') skills; rather than simply telling you what to do. We provide the methods for you to learn, consider, and adapt concepts to your unique situation. No one knows your library's personality or its standard procedures better than you. So you're the best one to decide what to include in screenings, orientations, training, and evaluations.

Examples from real life illustrate the application of ideas. Community service workers placed through a judicial system require an approach different from the one used to motivate and retain a retired businessman. Appropriate rewards and recognition vary by individual. We've included many items that work for us and others.

One section is devoted to academic, school, and special libraries. Their concerns are similar to those of public libraries, but their needs vary to an extent. We relay advice from those working in the field to jump-start your own approach.

All library people love stories, and we end the book with vignettes to help you deal with difficult or delicate situations, along with "character studies" of actual volunteer programs.

So there you have it—the complete (nearly so) guide to volunteerism in libraries. What do you supply? The energy, dedication, impetus, direction, judgment, discretion—in short, the humanity— which you already possess in abundance. You need nothing more to develop the very best volunteer effort for your library. Go to it.

◀1 BEGIN AT THE BEGINNING

A library without people is just a building full of books. Human beings give a library its reason for being. Patrons or customers are the primary group we consider. The concept of customer service is familiar to the library community. Equally important to the wise management of an institution are employee relations. The increased demands of customer relations have led management to rely more and more on a third group of people—volunteers. Yet, as libraries look to volunteers to alleviate problems, their well-being lags far behind in many institutions.

Volunteers offer unique benefits to any organization. They enhance and expand library resources, and add an element of fun to any work situation. They give added value for tax dollars.

However, in some agencies, volunteers are relegated to the most mundane tasks. At these libraries, the image of a typical volunteer conjures up an elderly, meek, maiden aunt sitting behind a desk and stamping overdue notices. This cliché contains about as much truth as the stereotype of a librarian. *"Usually more trouble than they're worth"* is the self-fulfilling prophecy at other institutions. Their reasons, admittedly based on experience, include unreliability, lack of skills and information, conflicts with paid staff, or self-centered attitudes.

To put this perspective into action, these libraries convey a distinct chill when a potential volunteer makes contact—there will be no cup of coffee, no regular desk, or even a hook to hang a coat on. Also there may be nonexistent or conflicting procedures, patronizing managers, and boring tasks causing volunteers to be a scarce commodity in these situations.

At the other extreme, you'll find libraries where volunteers rule like petty tyrants. In situations of political sensitivity, members of boards or commissions or advisory bodies may expropriate duties better suited to line staff because no one dares say "no."

In essence, a poor work environment never benefits the library or the volunteer. Volunteers are a resource that must be managed—and managed well—if they are to profit your library and gain satisfaction for themselves.

WHY BOTHER?

If there are so many ways to go astray when managing volunteers, why bother with them? We all have plenty of other priorities for work. Consider these reasons:

VOLUNTEERS INCREASE A LIBRARY'S CAPACITY TO PROVIDE NEEDED SERVICES.

This does not refer to basic services. We don't favor using volunteers to substitute for paid staff. We are referring to programs or projects that supplement or complement staff duties. These may be activities that have been designed from conception as primarily volunteer, or perhaps they are assistance in a pending crisis. Last, they might fall in the "wouldn't it be nice if we could" category. Examples of this "it would be nice" category include fund-raising dinners, presentations by authors, a move from an old building into a new facility, story times for kids at day care centers, tours of a library, computer classes for customers, used book sales, and calls to notify customers of requests.

Although paid staff can be used to mobilize any of these projects, in many instances involvement of volunteers frees employees to carry on day-to-day services and administrative duties. Effective volunteer use can extend the value of every dollar (tax or other) contributed in the community by providing increased labor.

VOLUNTEERS DIVERSIFY A LIBRARY'S HUMAN RESOURCES.

A library's staff frequently differs significantly from its customers or its community. Blend in a variety of volunteers—age, race, income, education, social strata—and you have an institution with a diversified public image. This evolution is in no way superficial. It extends to providing a continuous sampling of a community's opinions and feelings.

Volunteers bring skills that supplement or complement the salaried staff. These may be very specific, such as an artist painting a mural in the children's section. Or the talents may be less defined or anticipated, like a homemaker's newly-discovered ability to organize statistical reports.

VOLUNTEERS ADD THE ELEMENT OF ALTRUISM TO LIBRARY FUNCTIONS.

Day to day, library employees must address issues of funding, priorities, and management. We struggle to balance the demands of customers with never-ending job responsibilities. Daily scenarios may include the mediation of conflicts between co-workers; the next hour we might be repairing a photocopy machine or typewriter.

Much as an employee enjoys what he does, part of his motivation is money. Equally true, his actions and opinions are governed to some extent by the agency's policies and procedures. Only volunteers can cut through the differing, sometimes opposing, needs that cloud the successful fulfillment of every job. Only volunteers work for one reason—they want to serve.

With this image of altruism, volunteers increase the library's reputation for customer service. When a customer sees a neighbor helping out in your agency, you strengthen ties to your community and you personalize service.

VOLUNTEERS ARE A PUBLIC RELATIONS ASSET, BUILDING VISIBILITY AND CREDIBILITY—AND THEREFORE, SUPPORT—IN THE COMMUNITY.

A good volunteer program extends its impact far beyond the library. When satisfactory relationships exist between volunteers and an institution, the enthusiasm of the individuals generates a prevailing positive atmosphere. The information of their excitement, of the good work of the library, and of the many possibilities for service that exist is passed along to their friends and neighbors.

The results? More potential volunteers, burgeoning "buzz" about the library's good works, and avenues to fund-raising and political support. These effects, a plus at anytime, can be critical when competition increases for shares of government budgets. The corporate employee group you utilize today as cashiers at the book sale may become tomorrow's letter-writers to city council at budget review.

As spokespeople, volunteers are more believable than paid staff in the eyes of donors, customers, and legislators. And as private citizens, volunteers can voice their opinions to the public and the media with total impunity.

VOLUNTEERS BRING A NEW PERSPECTIVE AND AN EXHILARATION OF EXPERIMENTATION TO AN INSTITUTION.

Because they aren't part of the library establishment, volunteers look at an institution with a fresh vision. They can help when an issue or controversy arises, at the least by providing a trusted customer's point of view, at the most by applying problem-solving techniques you may not have considered. Thus they become agents of positive change in your library.

This same new perspective enables volunteers to experiment with new ideas, projects, and services. They can investigate a problem without excessive expense. For example, they can conduct a mini-marketing survey to determine if a new story time should be added, when, and for which specific age group.

VOLUNTEERING DEVELOPS INDIVIDUALS AS PRODUCTIVE MEMBERS OF THE COMMUNITY.

Crime, violence, suicide, alienation, frustration, anger, and stress have become hallmarks of our contemporary society. How can these be reduced or combated? There are many functions of volunteerism. The main purposes of volunteerism include providing people with opportunities to learn, grow, contribute, be part of a positive effort, shine as individuals, and struggle together as a team. As an institution whose roots are anchored firmly in the very heart of democracy, a library has a stake in its community. Supporting volunteerism is one method of being part of the solution.

WHAT? ME WORRY?

Okay, you're convinced of the value of a volunteer program. You have one already and want to improve it. Or you're thinking about starting one. Where do you go from here? Start with an organizational assessment. This is essentially a marketing or situational analysis of your current situation.

Try to enlist people from all levels and all areas of your library to complete the assessment. The objective is to gather information that provides a well-rounded picture of your library. By assembling demographics of your service area—for example educational level, ages, ethnic backgrounds, and so on—comparing this to your library's customers, you discover how they differ and are similar to the population at large.

These representations give you two clusters to compare to your current or anticipated volunteer needs. But before you start up a volunteer program, explore existing attitudes within your agency to determine how staff members feel about volunteers and if resources exist that support a volunteer program. Your library's short- and long-term objectives (for example, to increase circulation or to provide additional services to children) could have a major impact on the direction your volunteer program takes. This is the time to look realistically at your library's strengths and weaknesses, as well as your agency's major competitors who provide similar services or programs. See Figure 1-1: Organizational Assessment Worksheet.

FIGURE 1-1: Organizational Assessment Worksheet

ORGANIZATIONAL ASSESSMENT WORKSHEET

1. Describe your service area in terms of demographics like educational level, ages, ethnic backgrounds, etc.
2. Compare this to your library's customers. How are they different from and similar to the population at large?
3. Do you have a volunteer program? Describe it briefly.
4. How do staff members feel about volunteers?
5. What are your agency's major competitors? Consider businesses as well as education, information, entertainment providers. What are their strengths, weaknesses, and trends?
6. What are your library's short- and long-term objectives? How are these going to be reached? How will success be evaluated?
7. How are resources allocated?
8. Are suggestions, complaints, comments relayed from staff or the public to the administration? What happens to these?
9. What are your library's strengths? Are they being enhanced?
10. What are your library's weaknesses in general? How are they being handled?

STATEMENT OF PHILOSOPHY

The foundation of a volunteer program is the statement of philosophy. Like the Pledge of Allegiance or the Scouts' Code of Honor, a statement provides a strong base for the framework upon which you can develop goals, policies, and other decisions affecting volunteers in the organization. Be specific about why you are involving volunteers. For example:

> The Volunteer Office supplements and enhances services to the public through effective use of the talents, skills, and expertise of volunteers.

IF YOU HAVE A VOLUNTEER PROGRAM

If you currently have a volunteer program, you've already taken the first big step to success. But to ensure that your program is the best possible for your library, you need to appraise your current status. From an objective point of view, first gather information on the kind and numbers of present volunteers. Compare these to your customers and your community. Review your volunteer program. Consider the types of projects, activities, and responsibilities you give to volunteers. Are these related to specific objectives for your program and your library's overall development plans?

Maybe you wish you could attract more volunteers or a wider variety of people. Then you need to evaluate the competition for potential volunteers' time and think about what might attract them to your agency. Do you need to make changes in your recruitment techniques, or are more extensive modifications required? Perhaps you should offer more benefits.

Review the basics of your volunteer effort—budget, staffing patterns, office, work space, training and recruitment methods, the management structure, reward and recognition efforts. Start giving some thought to the future. Through formal and informal methods, you can gather opinions about unfulfilled needs that volunteers might provide at your library. By polling volunteers, you'll get ideas about where they think you should be heading. Summarize your strengths and weaknesses in dealing with volunteers.

VISUALIZE THE PROGRAM

Visualize what you would like your program to look like in six months, a year, two years. Begin attaching some specific goals and objectives, and developing a work plan. Make sure you include research needs such as assessments of staff and volunteer feedback.

A written survey or verbal interview gives you valuable insight into reasons why people volunteer, their perspective about your agency, how they first became involved, and why (or why not!) they continue. You should include demographic and lifestyle questions that help you in retention and recruitment efforts. Equally important is ascertaining the opinions of staff. They are the ones that set the tone for the library atmosphere, come up with tasks for volunteers, and provide the day-to-day supervision and contact. Involving staff gives them a stake in the outcome and the process helps you market your program to the decision-makers in your agency.

Figure 1-2 provides a method for your appraisal. If you decide you want in-depth information, such as a survey of volunteers or staff, this process should not slow down or discourage you. You can proceed with other elements of your program as you are planning for the more time-consuming matters.

FIGURE 1-2: What To Do If You Have A Volunteer Program

IF YOU HAVE A VOLUNTEER PROGRAM

1. What kind and numbers of people volunteer currently? Compare these to your customers and your community.
2. What projects, activities, programs are they involved with?
3. Do you have specific objectives for your program? How do these relate to your library's objectives?
4. What is the competition for your volunteers' time?
5. Who would you like to attract as volunteers? How do they differ from current ones?
6. What benefits do you provide to volunteers?
7. Do you have a budget? Paid staff?
8. At what locations and work spaces do volunteers work?
9. How do you recruit for volunteers and promote or publicize your program?
10. What needs are you filling for your library? For your volunteers?
11. What needs are you not meeting for your library? For your volunteers?
12. What would you like your program to look like in 6 months? 12 months? 18 months?
13. What research do you need?
14. Describe your training for volunteers. For staff who supervise volunteers.
15. Describe your reward and recognition efforts.
16. Who would make decisions about changes in your program (including expansion or reduction)?
17. What projects or duties do you have pending that might be filled by volunteers and why are these activities appropriate?
18. How are volunteers placed, or who determines their assignments?
19. How can volunteers express their opinions, suggestions, and complaints; and how do you respond to these?
20. Do you have a "career ladder" for volunteers?
21. Summarize your strengths in dealing with volunteers. Your weaknesses.
22. Make a diagram of the management structure for your volunteer program.

WHAT TO DO IF YOU DON'T HAVE A VOLUNTEER PROGRAM

You're the new kid on the block where volunteers are concerned and you want to set up a volunteer program, or you're just beginning. The organizational assessment gives you a snapshot of your library. Now let's move into more specifics about volunteers.

Start by considering exactly why you want a volunteer program. Perhaps you plan to expand your support base in the community in this fashion, or catch up on some long-neglected record keeping. Maybe your goals include expanding your outreach for the children's summer reading program or increasing ticket sales to a lecture. Although these specifics are nice, you need to probe for the broad motivations that underlie your plan. Do you anticipate that volunteers will supplement staff, or will they function independently, at least some of the time? Will they raise money? Serve as political advocates? Your responses will help determine the structure of your program and fit your objectives into the overall strategy and management of your library.

The next step is to consider what type of people will be interested in your potential program. They may match the demographics of your customers or your service area, and then again they may not. The more detailed your descriptions of the skills, background, and interests you need for particular aspects of your program, the more easily you can recruit.

STAFF INVOLVEMENT

Although the benefits that volunteers bring to an institution are attractive, a library must consider carefully the ways and types of their involvement. A pilot project enables staff the opportunity to become accustomed to volunteers, as well as permitting you to test recruitment, reporting, and recognition techniques. Staff involvement is critical to the success of this project. They should be pulled into the process; encouraged to brainstorm creative ways for volunteers to become involved in the library.

Explore the needs that may exist which volunteers might fill by asking staff and yourself:

- What services or activities do we provide now that we would like to increase?
- What other needs do our customers have that we presently can do nothing about?

- What unmet needs on the job does the staff have that volunteers might help with?
- What might we do differently if we had more skills or time?

As you go through this process, administrative concerns will begin to take shape. Employees will raise issues like management, day-to-day supervision, recruitment, training, placement, and evaluation. For a baseline upon which to measure future endeavors, you need to establish written goals and objectives, time lines, and summarize your possible strengths and weaknesses in dealing with volunteers.

The logical process for utilizing volunteers follows a sequence much like this:

- pinpoint where volunteers can be used,
- develop job descriptions with qualifications,
- publicize volunteer openings,
- interview and screen applicants,
- select appropriate volunteers and match with jobs,
- orient new volunteers to policies and practices,
- train new volunteers in specific jobs,
- track hours, duties, achievements, and
- evaluate activities.

Realistically, human beings don't always function quite so logically, and systems usually develop with an element of chance. Many libraries already have volunteers involved in some capacity, even if limited to organizing a small book sale or providing clerical support. This is fine if you've already gotten your feet wet, and you can go with the flow. In terms of building or strengthening your volunteer program, your most important task is to do something. Refining the specifics or improving management can occur simultaneously with involving volunteers.

In the final analysis, only two questions matter:

1. Does your library have the resources required to match the scope of the program you hope to establish?
2. Do the management and general staff of your library support the concept of a volunteer program?

If you can answer "yes" to both of these, any details can be worked out. Figure 1-3 will help you decide what directions may be most beneficial.

FIGURE 1-3: What To Do If You Don't Have A Volunteer Program

IF YOU DON'T HAVE A VOLUNTEER PROGRAM

1. What do you hope a volunteer program will accomplish?
2. What projects, activities, and programs could be worked on, and why are these especially appropriate for volunteers?
3. Do you have specific objectives for your program? How do these relate to your library's objectives?
4. What is the competition for possible volunteers?
5. Whom would you like to attract as volunteers?
6. What benefits can you provide to volunteers?
7. Do you have a budget? Paid staff?
8. How could you recruit volunteers and promote your program?
9. What realistic needs would volunteers fill for your library?
10. What would you like your program to look like in 6 months? 12 months? 18 months?
11. What research do you need?
12. Who would train your volunteers and what would that training include? For staff who supervise volunteers?
13. Who will make decisions about your program? How do these people envision its structure, role, management?
14. Diagram a possible management and supervision structure for your program, with duties like recruitment, training, placement.
15. How would volunteers express their opinions, suggestions, and complaints; and how could you respond to these?
16. Summarize your strengths and weaknesses with volunteers.

GOALS AND OBJECTIVES

Good management of any type requires creation of goals and objectives. A well-run volunteer program is no different. *"Goals"* are broad statements of purpose—what you plan to achieve. *"Objectives"* are the methods by which you will reach goals and should be measurable in some fashion.

But numbers aren't necessarily the best measurement. Numerical targets for volunteers are meaningless unless serious expectations of productivity are also elucidated, along with quality of activities and support for overall goals. Consider the following questions:

- What do we expect individual volunteers to accomplish in each job category?
- What type of diversity do we want represented in our volunteer program?

- What response should customers have to the service they receive from volunteers?
- What effect do we want volunteers to have in special assignments, such as public education, etc.?
- What outreach efforts do we expect our director of volunteers to make this year?

Goals and objectives set for the volunteer component should correlate with the overall goals and objectives of your library. Include volunteers in your plans for future library projects. Involve the director of volunteers in comprehensive agency planning.

This process may seem like an overwhelming task, but in fact you probably are accomplishing it in some fashion already. Let's take a typical library volunteer activity — sponsoring an annual evening of appearances by local writers. You have records on the numbers of volunteers you deployed as ushers last year and whether that was too few, too many, or just right. You also have an idea about the quality and amount of training. More training might result in a need for fewer volunteers or better service to those attending. Your goals and objectives quite logically and simply flow from the activity. They might be stated like the following:

GOAL: To host an hospitable and successful evening with local authors by providing volunteer support.

OBJECTIVE 1: Recruit twenty volunteers to sell tickets, usher, and clean up after the event.

OBJECTIVE 2: Train ten volunteers as ushers to seat audience members efficiently, on time, and in an orderly fashion.

OBJECTIVE 3: Provide all volunteers with a minimum level of information about the authors who are appearing so that they can answer basic questions.

OBJECTIVE 4: Ensure that volunteers selling tickets are fiscally responsible and know the basic rules of sales.

OBJECTIVE 5: Expand the library's impact by distributing flyers about Library Week to the audience.

Each objective can be supported by a series of steps, or an action plan, and can be accomplished relatively easily. But the identical process is also used for broader goals and year-to-year planning. The element critical to include is the one most forgotten — final evaluation. Did you actually attain your objectives and to what extent?

Recycle the goals, objectives, and evaluations back into your regular planning sequence. They become the basis for the next series of efforts. Figure 1-4 is an example of a Work and Action Plan.

FIGURE 1-4: A Work And Action Plan

A WORK AND ACTION PLAN

List three to five broad goals for the volunteer program as well as several specific, measurable objectives for each.

Example of goal:
Within six months, create a workable structure for the volunteer program.

1.
2.
3.
4.
5.

Example of objectives to support the goal:
- Meet with branch managers to obtain their perspective and agreement on day-to-day supervision.
- Brainstorm with staff about possible volunteer projects; select several that reasonably can be achieved in the time period.
- Establish a system to track individuals, hours, and duties.

POLICY DEVELOPMENT

Have you ever attended a meeting that lacked an effective chairperson and an agenda? The usual results are confusion and chaos, meandering conversations, and a sense of dissatisfaction. Policies for volunteer involvement in your library provide leadership and direction in much the same manner that parliamentary procedure and a chairperson do. They furnish a framework that everyone understands. When people understand the rules, they can either follow them or work to change them. Without regulations, expectations are unknown, everyone operates independently, and standards are unenforceable.

Whether stated as such or compiled in a handbook, a policy decision is required to recruit volunteers initially and to allocate resources to their support.

Your library may favor formality and officially ratify subsequent management directives, such as recording volunteer hours or requiring a formal application. More likely, you'll find yourself using a combination of forethought and applied experience to develop preferred practices.

Make sure all new (and veteran) employees know the standards that have been set and be alert to new situations that require revision of policies about volunteers. The establishment and application of policies involving volunteers are two of the most visible ways you can demonstrate commitment to the integration of volunteers into your library. The following is an example of a broad policy:

> Volunteer services are the means by which the library extends and enhances services to customers. The purposes of the volunteer services program are to supplement the efforts of paid library staff to meet demands for quality customer service; to serve as a method for citizens to become familiar with the library; and to provide an opportunity for citizens to volunteer and make positive contributions to their quality of life.

ORGANIZATIONAL PLACEMENT

The position of the head of the volunteer program in your library's organization chart indicates how—even whether—volunteers are part of the organization. Often the director of volunteers is a separate, independent department head whose responsibilities differ from those of all other departments. She is linked throughout the agency and impacts the efficacy of services through a large cadre of workers that she supervises. Other logical locations for the director are within human resources or public relations.

Members of boards and commissions that have legal authority and responsibility are at the top of the hierarchy. The volunteer office is shown parallel to other management-level positions, under the departments in which they function. Volunteers are channeled to the appropriate department and branches where daily supervision is provided. An example of the Denver Public Library's organization chart can been seen in Figure 1-5.

LEGAL ISSUES

Legal matters concerning volunteers can be serious. Laws vary from state to state, and from time to time. Our purpose is to offer general advice and guidelines, not to give absolute answers. You should consult your library's chief executive and other experts to ensure that you are complying with local ordinances and policies.

FIGURE 1-5: Denver Public Library Organization Chart

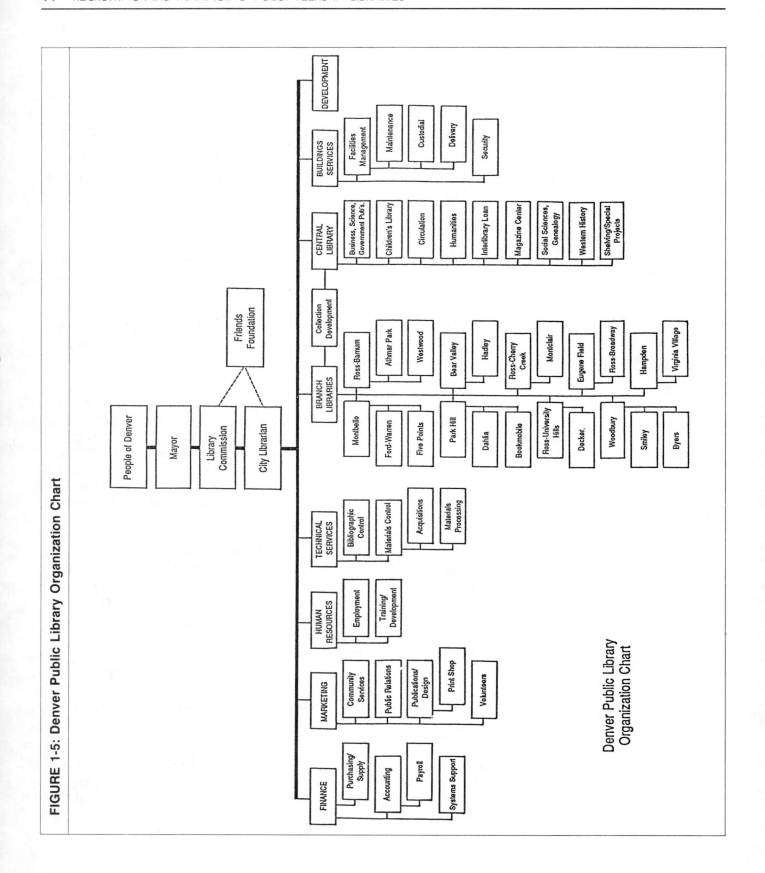

Denver Public Library
Organization Chart

Don't forget your common sense, too. An ounce of prevention goes a long way toward preventing problems, even if it's not required by a written law.

RISK AND PERSONAL INJURY

Volunteers are not usually covered under the Workman's Compensation Act if injured while performing their volunteer duties. They are not treated as paid employees in this case. Volunteers and board members may be covered by current insurance for liability if they are authorized by the library to perform a service. In this instance, they are like paid employees.

A library may represent a volunteer in a claim or lawsuit as long as the agency's attorney determines that the volunteer was acting within the course and scope of volunteer duty and was not acting in a willful or wanton manner. A library normally does not represent a volunteer when the volunteer is acting improperly. These guidelines also apply to members of boards and commissions. Many agencies now are obtaining special insurance to protect volunteers from lawsuits, liability and other concerns. Two primary areas of focus are governing boards and special events.

USE OF VEHICLES

Normally volunteers retain personal liability when they use their own cars for library business. They are responsible for damages to their car or other autos, or injury to other people. It is very important the library ascertain that volunteers provide complete accident and liability coverage for their vehicles. They may want to obtain a rider on their personal insurance policy to cover any damages that occur on library business.

RECORDS

Any on-the-job accident, sudden illness, or injury should be promptly reported to a staff member. If your library uses an accident form or particular reporting methods, you should implement these for volunteers just as you do paid employees. In the absence of a printed questionnaire, prepare your own brief written statement and send duplicates to the security, personnel, and volunteer offices. The best insurance is prevention, so avoid high risk situations.

Volunteers always should provide the name of a person to contact in case of emergency. This information, often initially located on the volunteer application, becomes part of the individual's permanent file and should be updated periodically.

SCREENING VOLUNTEERS

Some volunteers work in situations that have potential for sensitive interaction. People who visit the elderly or incapacitated in their homes or those with frequent and independent association with children are two examples. As part of the screening process we ask for a security clearance in such instances through the Colorado Bureau of Investigation and similar agencies. You may want to explore the clearances you prefer. Further discussion on screening volunteers will occur in a later chapter. Most candidates for the volunteer program will understand the reason for a thorough process when you explain your organization's concerns that customers be served and protected.

VOLUNTEERS ARE NOT "FREE" LABOR

All volunteer programs require financial support as well as intellectual commitment. While resources differ from institution to institution, don't shortchange yourself with unrealistic budget considerations.

STAFF

Ideally the director of volunteers is a full-time professional, trained in management and strong in people skills. But whether your library manages with a volunteer, a part-time position, combines supervision of volunteers with additional duties, or is fortunate enough to have a full-time director, that individual should be at the management level.

The job of director of volunteers requires decision-making, leadership, and a great deal of public contact on behalf of your library. The salary for this position should correlate to its professional demands. Consider what you are paying other department heads or key administrative employees. Based on the size or schedule of your volunteer program, the personnel budget could include the program's secretary and any additional assistants necessary to operate.

OTHER RESOURCES

Other operational costs and needed resources impact your bottom line. Some may already be available. Others you may need to budget for. A sample checklist is provided—Complete it to ensure that everything that is needed is accounted for.

Space and other facilities: The office (some functions may be shared space) should include:

____ Easy access from the entrance of the building.
____ Privacy for interviewing prospective volunteers.
____ Storage space that is secure for volunteers' coats and other personal belongings.
____ Group work space to permit meetings, mailings, collating of materials, etc.
____ Orientation and in-service training space.
____ Volunteer work space.
____ Access to staff room (rest area) and restroom.

Furniture and equipment:

____ Chairs, coat rack, bulletin boards, file cabinets
____ Typewriters, computers, access to equipment such as telefaxes, calculators (Note that many clerical staff object to sharing typewriters or computers because it interferes with their work)
____ Slide projector and screen, videocassette monitor (for recruitment, orientation, and training)
____ Comfortable furniture for conversation/interview or lounge space
____ Telephone (essential for recruitment and constant communication with volunteers and staff)
____ Supplies: Budget for supplies should be calculated on the basis of the needs of both the volunteer office and the volunteers themselves. The amount of supplies will rise as the number of active volunteers increase.
____ Paper and stationery
____ Pencils, pens, typewriter ribbons, paper clips
____ Hospitality items such as coffee, tea, cups, paper towels, napkins

Printing and reproduction: The major expenditure for the volunteer program, especially during the first year. Do you have—or need—these items?

____ Volunteer applications
____ Record-keeping forms
____ Recruitment brochures, flyers, posters
____ Recognition certificates
____ Invitations for events
____ Volunteer newsletter or bulletin
____ Training materials and handbooks

Postage: Varies depending on your program. Review your annual work plan for mailing needs related to recruitment and activities such as festivals, special presentations in the library, and major projects, multiplied by the length of various mailing lists.

Recognition: To thank volunteers and the staff who supervise them. Budget can be small or large but should include some amount for recognition—party, inexpensive certificates of appreciation, small gift items (such as mugs, t-shirts, pencils, pens, notebooks, notecards, books).

Travel: The cost of getting to presentations throughout the community. Government agencies usually have a standard mileage rate that applies. Travel also should accommodate trips to state and national meetings or conferences.

Professional development: Funds for memberships in various professional societies both for the volunteer office staff and for key volunteers. Volunteerism journal subscriptions and book purchases for an in-house library. Training ranging from speaker fees to video rentals, books, handout materials, and conferences or workshops.

VOLUNTEER PROGRAM NEEDS

Every volunteer program has unique needs. Often the volunteer office has requests that seem strange in the library world. What other department would purchase streamers and confetti?! Hire a rock-and-roll band? Order two hundred teeny flashlights? The creative aspects of recruitment, motivation, and recognition require supplies that set a tone or atmosphere different from the rest of the library. And funds expended on volunteers are leveraged into more hours and types of service than the same amount of money would pay for in salaried personnel.

Time spent in planning for volunteers ensures that your house is in order before you open the doors to recruit. If the public sees your library's volunteer program managed effectively, volunteers will be eager to join you.

RESOURCES

Books:

From the Top Down: the executive role in volunteer program success. Ellis, Susan; Energize Associates; Philadelphia, Pennsylvania; 1986.

The Effective Management of Volunteer Programs. Wilson, Marlene; Johnson Publishing Company; Boulder, Colorado; 1979.

Managing Nonprofit Organizations in the 21st Century. Gelatt, James P.; Oryx Press; Phoenix, Arizona; 1992.

Motivating and Managing Today's Volunteers: how to build and lead a terrific team. MacLeod, Flora; International Self-Counsel Press Ltd; Bellingham, Washington; 1993.

Recruiting Volunteers. Burke, Mary Ann; Crisp Publications; Los Altos, California; 1992.

Stand Up and Be Counted: the volunteer resource book. Knipe, Judy; Simon and Schuster; New York; 1992.

Training Strategies from Start to Finish. Friedman, Paul G., and Yarbrough, Elaine A.; Prentice-Hall Inc.; Englewood Cliffs, New Jersey; 1986.

You Can Make a Difference: helping others and yourself through volunteering. Wilson, Marlene; Volunteers Management Associates; Boulder, Colorado; 1990.

Journals and Newsletters:
Grapevine, VM Systems/Heritage Arts, 1807 Prairie Avenue, Downers Grove, Illinois 60515.

The Journal of Volunteer Administration, P. O. Box 4584, Boulder, Colorado 80306.

Organizations:
Association for Volunteer Administration, P. O. Box 4584, Boulder, Colorado 80306; 303/541-0238.

Directors of Volunteers in Agencies, P. O. Box 18941, Denver, Colorado 80218-0941; 303/727-7957.

2 RECRUITMENT AND TRENDS

Libraries live in competitive times, not only for financial support but also for volunteer assistance. A 1993 national survey by Scripps Howard News Service and Ohio University found that only one-third of adults in the nation worked for a charity or any other kind of local nonprofit group in the last month. Americans feel they are too busy. Demands on their time and energy are enormous. Even traditional avenues of service like Kiwanis Clubs or parent-teacher organizations, the survey found, have dwindling numbers of volunteers.

Take heart! The changing, competitive atmosphere actually offers libraries a window of opportunity. We frequently have longer hours, varied locations, and an ambiance of personal initiative that makes us appealing to today's independent, well-educated, busy population. We do have to be street savvy as well as analytical when we embark on recruitment efforts.

WHAT DO VOLUNTEERS REALLY WANT?

No matter how slick your promotional materials or smooth your techniques, the bottom line for volunteer managers is—do people volunteer? Are they motivated to make the critical initial call or contact? (This question is separate from the factors that keep them coming back.)

Volunteers may be unaware of their motivations. But if you can identify the reasons, you'll increase your success in recruiting the right people for specific tasks. Almost no one volunteers simply because you're a worthy cause. Those exist by the thousands. Nor is a love of books necessarily the common denominator. People interested solely in books prefer to sit around reading rather than volunteering.

Consider the types of personalities that might match an activity and position your recruitment materials to reflect these. One or more of the following may provide the motivation for a successful volunteer experience:

1. Social interaction/friendship: Does your project offer the opportunity for human contact? How much and what type? Many people take a first volunteer step because they want to make new acquaintances.

2. High visibility/potential for recognition: Social, government, and business leaders frequently prefer activities that enable them to shine in the public eye.

3. Management challenge: Organizers, builders, and engineers, sign up here! These folks thrive when pulling together a project from the bottom up.

4. Mental stimulation: You hear this reason from young mothers isolated at home or people with routine jobs. They want a challenge that keeps their minds from rusting but not necessarily one that requires a major time commitment.

5. Unraveling a puzzle: Those with a scientific, explorer's curiosity frequently find their needs supplied by research projects or activities with many details.

6. Service to humanity: The passionate idealist can spread his commitment to literacy, literature, and libraries by moving past words into action.

7. Occupy time: The backbone of many volunteer efforts, these are the folks who happily stuff envelopes and sit at festival booths simply to keep busy. They'd probably do the same for any worthy cause; yours happens to be the lucky one.

8. Affiliation with peers: If you remember joining the Scouts or a church youth group because "everyone's doing it," you have the key to another strong motivator. Friends, relatives, and co-workers frequently heavily influence others to volunteer.

Bottom line—several recent studies give us an overview of lifestyle traits that increase an individual's potential to be a volunteer. These include attending religious services; ages between thirty-five and retirement; paid employment; and higher levels of education. Do your current volunteers match? Can you use these indicators to refine your recruitment methods?

HOW TO RECRUIT

Assuming you have a wish list of tasks, jobs, projects, and activities as high as you can reach, how do you find the people who might volunteer? In brief, you think like the type of individual you're trying to attract. You put yourself in this mind-set to project how he might be reached and what might attract her into making that critical call to you.

Recruitment breaks down into several segments—media, individual, and personal. Each offers advantages and disadvantages based on your resources and needs along with those of your potential volunteers.

Remember to partner each and every recruitment method with one or more of the eight motivators previously described. This can be accomplished through brief job descriptions, photos and art, slogans, and just plain conversation. Recruitment is inexact. You can be inundated with volunteers at one moment and absolutely solitary the next. By utilizing the full range of recruitment techniques, you can help level out the extremes.

PERSONAL RECRUITMENT

Word-of-mouth advertising, while sometimes time-consuming, is most effective in attracting a potentially very loyal and dedicated corps. Because it's conducted between acquaintances, the recruitment is tailored to the exact requirements of each person, and the appeal is based on characteristics attractive or important to him—even guilt! ("I helped you with your project. Now come help me with my favorite.")

One mother brought her daughter to participate in a kazoo band that performs at library special events. An employee's mother-in-law began regular hours in an office after her husband passed away. A senior staff member persuaded her church group to give her a hand with mailings. In any case, even with personal appeals, you and other staff or current volunteers will find it helpful to have some sort of listing or announcement of types of duties to review. That way, you can tempt people with a variety or solicit special skills. Obviously, personal recruitment frequently is most successful with people swayed by social, visibility, recognition, and filling-time motivators.

INDIVIDUAL RECRUITMENT

This method relies on one-to-one contact but through a means such as a mailing, a flyer at a library or some other site, or a presentation to a group. You can reach small or large numbers of people in this fashion and target the types or skills you need.

An especially valuable group that can be contacted are the ones currently in your volunteer pool. Depending upon your record-keeping system, you may be able to pinpoint volunteers who live in a particular neighborhood, have an interest in ushering at an event, or are free during the day. Consider these types of outlets for individual recruitment:

- posters at stores, shopping centers, businesses, churches, community centers,
- flyers at library circ desks,
- notices in church, school, or business newsletters,
- mailings (either on your own or piggy-backed with another group),
- contacts to employee service organizations,
- speeches to groups whose programs or goals complement yours—book talk groups, student organizations, genealogy researchers and,
- corporate bulletin boards.

MEDIA RECRUITMENT

The broadest, least targeted type of recruitment is through the media. You can reach the largest possible number of potential volunteers this way. However, as a group, members of the general public are least likely to possess specific skills and the most likely to abandon their initiative. This method also requires you to perform an inordinate amount of interviewing and evaluating to place the recruit.

Its advantages? It is especially useful to obtain large numbers of volunteers for relatively short-term, unskilled work forces, such as mailings, book sales, and ushering. It also works to help you tap into new markets of recruits you haven't been able to reach before and to promote activities with lots of popular emotional appeal, such as projects serving children or the elderly. Last, it gives visibility to your library and your volunteer program even if it gains you no volunteers at all.

If you have the time and the resources, you should tailor information to the particular interests of the medium you're attempting to reach through its audience. Keep in mind deadlines, time and space restrictions, geographic distribution, and other special interests.

Newspapers

In most cases, editors or reporters working with feature articles, announcements, or event calendars are the people you are trying to reach rather than news or editorial staff. Especially valuable are smaller publications. Try slanting your release to seniors for a senior publication; include a reference to a local branch library in a neighborhood newspaper.

Radio

Limit yourself to one or two brief job descriptions and about 100 words. Send these to the public service or community affairs director.

Television

Only one announcement at a time, with 25 words. Because competition for television time is so intensive, save this outlet for occasional use only. *Don't forget cable television.* This is a growing area of viewership, and you often can get your messages used far more frequently than on the airwaves.

The heart of your contacts with the media is the same information you used in bulletins or flyers. It is reformatted slightly to fit the media's needs.

Interviews/Articles

A word about interviews or longer articles—if your library has a public relations manager or if you have the time to try to get this type of coverage yourself, it combines aspects of reward and recognition with recruitment. Although competition for coverage in the mass media is intense, you often can get good results by matching a volunteer, a project, or activities to a specific outlet or reporter. For example, reporters with children sometimes respond well to story ideas that focus on children. A controversial talk show host might go for a guest discussing a volunteer project that reaches at-risk teens.

THE RECRUITMENT NOTICE

The foundation of volunteer recruitment is a written notice. Based on job descriptions (whether long or short, written or unwritten), the notice contains brief essentials of each volunteer position. Because its purpose is to attract potential volunteers, it makes its listings attractive while including requirements or restrictions, such as hours work must be performed, length of commitment, and so on.

The notice can be reproduced and distributed. Make sure you are aware that too many choices may overwhelm the reader. We suggest not more than four or five for each notice. In the personal interview, you can mention additional opportunities that may be attractive to a particular person.

Notices can be issued at regular intervals or for special projects. They also can be adapted to specific locations. By designing a standard "masthead" to announce volunteer openings, it's easy to modify notices for regular or targeted mailings. The notice is also the basis for news releases. Remember, your goal again is to encourage people to contact you, not to convey each and every detail. Bright, upbeat, interesting writing helps. And, of course, try to capture an element that will motivate the particular volunteers you need. See Figures 2-1 and 2-2 for examples of bulletins.

TRENDS IN VOLUNTEER MANAGEMENT

For decades, volunteerism outside of the church or school primarily appealed to middle-class women. A social opportunity, a personal challenge, a method to utilize their intelligence and skills, volunteerism fit around their family needs and helped define their own identity at the same time. Governing boards of institutions were an exception where business executives brushed shoulders with male representatives of leading families or prominent civic leaders.

Volunteers were available during the day. Because they didn't necessarily expect a high degree of responsibility, they willingly assumed even the most mundane tasks, happily arranged parties, and poured tea.

Yet times and people have changed. The *traditional* volunteer is gone. Only ten percent of the population fits the stereotype of unemployed, available, homemaker. The volunteer force is feeling the impact of changes in lifestyles, such as single parents, two working parents, growing percentage of seniors and ethnic minorities, nontraditional students, and other people with special needs.

These changes in our fast-paced, high-stress society mean changes in all aspects of managing volunteers, from recruitment to training, volunteer projects to scheduling. Consider the five major trends in volunteerism that should guide your recruitment efforts:

1. **BREAK STEREOTYPES: VOLUNTEERS COME IN ALL SHAPES AND SIZES.** With the decline of "traditional" volunteers, don't lose heart. You have limitless sources of new and diverse people if you open your own eyes and the minds of your co-workers.

Seniors are skilled and reliable, and people over the age of 60

FIGURE 2-1: Volunteer Bulletin

Volunteer Opportunities

AT THE DENVER PUBLIC LIBRARY

WINTER 1994

ENRICH YOUR LIFE BY VOLUNTEERING

Volunteers come with all sorts of interests. At the Denver Public Library, you can choose the kind of activity and time that suit you best. Think about some of these fun-filled and challenging options:

BOOKWORM: Clown around with kids and books? Yes, indeed, we're recruiting frustrated hams, late-blooming actors, and erst-while comics to assume the Bookworm's costume. You'll appear at festivals and fairs, parties, story hours and other events. Chat with children, read stories, give away stickers and library info. We especially need volunteers who are available during week days.

READ ALOUD: Make magic with reading for the Read Aloud Program. People from all backgrounds, especially those who read Spanish, are welcome. You complete a two-hour training session (in February) and read to an assigned group of preschool children at least once a week for eight to ten weeks, during school hours in Denver.

BAR-CODING: High tech hits the Library! Help us speed up the book-check-out process. Put new labels on books and enter numeric data on computer. Time commitment is a minimum of two hours a week for at least three months.

BOOK SALE BOOK-SORTER: Hard-core bibliophiles sought for year-round work sorting books for the annual Used Book Sale. If you've got broad knowledge of books, we'll train you to search and separate. You should be available on Tuesdays and Thursdays during daytime hours.

"MARIAN, THE LIBRARIAN" SCHOOL HOT LINE: Put your mouth where your mouth is! Encourage young adults to stay in school by providing library help. You'll answer the hot line phone, locate the books they need, and organize materials for delivery. This is a new project at Ford-Warren and Montbello branches in cooperation with Denver Public Schools.

OFFICE AIDE: Regular help is always needed with typing, word processing, filing, and mailings. If you love talking on the phone, you can call about reserves and activities.

For more information, call 640-8958.
(TDD for persons with hearing impairments, 640-8980.)

FIGURE 2-2: Volunteer Bulletin

Volunteer Opportunities
AT THE DENVER PUBLIC LIBRARY

You can choose the kind of activity and the times that best suit you. Fun filled, challenging options listed below.

Location

Ross-Broadway
Branch Library
33 E. Bayaud Ave.
at S. Lincoln St.
Denver, 80209

Hampden Branch
Library
9755 E. Girard Ave.
at S. Dayton St.
Denver, 80231

Marketing Department
Library Admin. Center
1330 Fox St.
Denver, 80204

Central Library
1357 Broadway
Denver, 80203

Immediate Openings

TELEPHONE CALLER: "Your book is in!" is music to the ears of a customer awaiting their special request for library material. Need a commitment of 2 hours a day twice a week. Training provided. Yes, you'll be among the first to see best sellers and other hot items.

LIBRARY AIDE: Be part of the team that does it all. Create order out of chaos where needed. Help with extra stamping, stapling, sorting, straightening shelves, calling, converting periodicals, labeling, routing books and more.

Like people? Got a knack for organization? Looking for long term marketing projects? Help needed for many jobs related to opening the new Central Library. Here is an opportunity to be involved with a busy, exciting office. Training provided, flexible hours.

Circulation Department: Needs telephone callers, and help with book returns. Training begins in February. Requires at least two hours twice a week.

Genealogy Department: Needs volunteers to train new customers with beginning genealogy searches. Training provided, flexible schedule available.

If you'd like to participate in any of these tasks please call Terry Nelson at 640-8957.

TDD telecommunications device for persons with hearing impairments: 640-8980

THE DENVER PUBLIC LIBRARY

are a burgeoning percentage of our population; most of them are as active today as they were yesterday. To many of these people, leisure time is designed to fill with worthwhile activities. They were raised on a service philosophy.

Local courts may serve as the origin for an unending stream of unpaid assistance. Many judicial systems now order community service as an alternative or complement to fines or prison. This source is, by definition, short-term. While you probably wouldn't want to place people convicted of violent or major infractions, you might be able to use others after carefully screening and matching. (See Chapter 7 on community service placements.)

Other areas? Minority groups and persons with disabilities always have been underutilized in libraries. To lay a foundation for recruitment with these individuals, libraries should increase their visibility in special communities. It may seem strange for volunteer recruitment to begin at a street fair or conference, but these and similar community events provide contacts and initiate relationships. Build around local celebrations like African-American arts festivals and Cinco de Mayo. Use volunteers and staff who are members of the special groups to lead, plan, and staff the event to ensure that people with multicultural heritages know they have associates at the library. You can increase your impact by preparing special publications like book lists or hosting related events and displays.

With the commencement of the Americans with Disabilities Act, all our facilities are becoming more accessible. This provides an opportunity to involve persons with disabilities (or "differently-abled") as volunteers, too. Potential sources include schools and service agencies, as well as regular outlets.

Students with disabilities, like all students, want "real life situations" to test their skills. Adults seek the same sense of fulfillment as other volunteers. Differently-abled volunteers have performed such diverse tasks as technical research, painting, and book repair.

2. **SERVE THE CORPORATE COMMUNITY WHILE IT HELPS YOU.** Businesses often lead their communities in good citizenship, and good citizens care about their town, state, country. Business executives realize that volunteer efforts help improve the quality of life for everyone. They also know that "good works" position their firms for increased visibility, ultimately affecting the bottom line. No wonder the management philosophy at many firms actively encourages volunteering.

Individual employees get a pay-off, too. In addition to self-satisfaction, volunteer experience demonstrates personal qualities like initiative and commitment that are desirable for promotions.

Some corporations and agencies encourage their formal groups of employees—such as staff councils or specially formed service groups—to become active in volunteer work. These groups prefer projects that identify them as an association, in which they work together to build affinity. For example, at the DPL's book sale, the corporation's CEO can sit next to one of his own clerical staff to ring up purchases, an informal and nonthreatening atmosphere in which to become better acquainted. Most important, employees, whether alone or as a group, seek opportunities they can't get at work. These might be as simple as social contacts or as challenging as managing a complex project.

To recruit volunteers from the business community, you must carefully assess their needs. Do they want high visibility? Place them in positions with lots of interaction with the public and media. Are they matching the volunteer project with a corporate goal, such as assistance on literacy? Do they hope they can participate with their families? Unless libraries can provide such opportunities, they'll miss out on these volunteers.

Businesses frequently have a formal process by which they accept a volunteer project. They evaluate the nonprofit group, looking for the same accountability and good management they seek in the corporate community. They consider structure, training for volunteers, planning, and the human, caring touch. They may require a written and/or verbal presentation of volunteer opportunities, have a written timetable, or compare your request to a list of their priorities.

Try cultivating an advocate within the corporation to find out its procedures and help you make the appeal, whether your need is for an individual, group involvement, or to present a variety of opportunities. This shows a degree of support already exists in the employee base and that support may grow, too. An executive serving on your board of directors can be a conduit to additional volunteers, in-kind support like equipment, even grants and funding.

3. **PROVIDE CAREER PERSPECTIVES AND JOB SKILLS ALONG WITH VOLUNTEER EXPERIENCE.** Let's be realistic. People no longer anticipate staying in the same occupation their entire working life. Indeed, they see this possibility as positively boring. Predictions say we'll make career shifts several times before we retire. Young people have even more challenges. Not only do they lack practical experience, but also they frequently are ignorant about types of jobs that exist. In addition, by choice

or chance, they may have missed educational opportunities in school.

No matter what our age or occupation, volunteerism provides information on options, training, and experience that can profit us professionally. Volunteer program managers should flaunt these benefits in publications, presentations, and interviews.

The contention for youth: "service learning" gives them practical, hands-on experience. They can test a skill or learn a new one, gain a realistic view of the work world. Some school programs are beginning to require community service as a prerequisite for graduation. The DPL has utilized students fulfilling graduation requirements for specialized degrees, interns (paid or unpaid) in a variety of fields, and work-study students.

On top of the practical, volunteer experience fosters a philosophy of giving back to the community, a giving of self that can be more important than money or position. Ultimately these positive feelings result in self-esteem and confidence, important to success in any job.

For students with behavioral problems, volunteering can make a world of difference. Here they can shed an undeserved or undesired reputation. Here they learn that they count as a person and matters of their clothes, make-up, or school status are secondary. They can practice reading and writing, reach out to little children or seniors, stand on their own feet. Volunteering improves their self-image and gives them a work record upon which to base a resume and references.

The position for adults: Other people who can relate volunteerism to job skills are the unemployed (fills in gaps in their employment history), homemakers seeking to return to the job market, or people wishing to make career changes. Two young mothers might share a volunteer position, split baby-sitting costs, and both hone their skills and make job contacts.

Libraries should remember that these volunteers don't intend to be around forever. Be candid about your needs and explore the recruits' with them. Define the beginning and ending of their volunteer tasks. Use them to manage short-term special programs. This will enable them to refine their data entry skills and together establish desired results for a project.

4. GIVE VOLUNTEERS WHAT THEY REALLY WANT— THE HUMAN TOUCH. In an increasingly automated, frantic, impersonal society, your greatest appeal for individuals may very well be human beings. The most popular volunteer efforts at the Denver Public Library are those where people work with other people—in teams, in small committees, or large groups. Nowadays, so much time is spent with machines—computers, telephones, photocopy and telefax machines, production equipment—that we can go an entire day without seeing another human. Even our phone calls are answered by automated services.

Volunteer efforts that provide direct, personal interaction rank high in desirability. The DPL's popular Homebound Service depends on regular visits between the volunteer and senior. An eight-week commitment for volunteers participating in the Read Aloud Program creates no problems because readers mingle with preschoolers. Even routine work like sorting used books is tolerated because of the camaraderie built among the volunteer committee members. High touch is essential in a world based on high tech.

5. **CHANGE WITH THE CHANGING TIMES.** Today's differing lifestyles mandate two qualities in volunteer programs: flexibility and professionalism.

Flexibility means a variety of opportunities, not just routine or route work. A retired businessman, like the one who managed the DPL's Homebound Service for two years, needs a real challenge, responsibility, and authority to make the program a success. A man whose life-long avocation has been rare books must be given scope to exercise that skill, like the lay expert who volunteers for the DPL's Rare Book Auction.

The best way to discover these needs? Ask a volunteer what her interests and background are. Give him choices. Offer activities that utilize their skills and provide personal fulfillment.

Flexibility in hours and locations is a natural extension of trends in volunteerism. Libraries have an edge in this regard because they often stay open during non-business hours and have facilities in various neighborhoods.

Clearly, a library must be able to respond to these requirements. This requires professionalism. None of us can afford round-the-clock specialty staff to manage volunteers. While the manager of a volunteer's schedule must be flexible to handle special events and activities, also consider a support corps. You may select key staff members (or they may volunteer) to be the volunteer contact in their department or branch. Be sure to provide additional training and support to these folks.

Professionalism mandates continual efforts in training for volunteers; rules and policies that govern library staff and volunteers equitably; recruitment techniques; statistics and reporting. Professionalism places another charge on libraries—money. Libraries must be willing to invest in their volunteers. Recruitment, training, recognition and management of volunteers aren't free. (See Chapter 1, for more information about financial needs).

COLLABORATION

One trend is so innovative that it deserves separate mention—that is, collaboration. The word crops up in many conversations these days, from staff meetings to strategic planning sessions, at agencies of similar or widely varying missions.

Nonprofit agencies in the past had limited contact with one another. Their reluctance at times sprang from a feeling of competition for volunteers and financial support. No more. Cooperative efforts—or collaboration—are increasingly important because they stretch resources and save money.

Formal and informal associations with other managers of volunteers and with the far-flung network of nonprofit and community-oriented businesses lead to many opportunities. Shared training programs, combined recruitment through advertising and promotional campaigns, and jointly staffed activities like booths at fairs and festivals are just a few ideas.

In the Denver metro area, local libraries began sending their managers of volunteers to regular meetings in 1993. From that they shared ideas and concerns, initiated a media campaign for Library Week and Volunteer Week, and began a handbook to help each other.

Another benefit—collaboration appeals to potential funders who feel that cooperative efforts are more businesslike and cost-effective. These might be reflected in a grant request, like the community art project created by volunteers at a DPL branch library. Three neighborhood organizations pledged their involvement and were the deciding factor in obtaining the final funding.

Some projects are undergoing development by two or more nonprofit groups. For example, the DPL is working with the Denver Art Museum and the Colorado Historical Society in the innovative Civic Center Cultural Complex that will include complementary exhibits, activities, staff, and volunteer efforts.

TRAINING PROGRAMS

Volunteer managers of agencies with complementary interests in education and culture joined together to share expenses to bring a nationally renowned trainer for a volunteer workshop. The Denver Art Museum, Museum of Natural History, Colorado History Museum, Denver Zoo, and the Denver Public Library provided an opportunity for staff development that none could have justified on its own.

The training also was offered to lead or key volunteers as volunteer recognition as well as development. Because the session was held during National Volunteer Week, it spotlighted the important role that volunteers fill in the nonprofit world.

CROSS-REFERRALS

Experts in volunteerism know that a volunteer with nothing to do, or a volunteer misplaced in a position, doesn't stay around for long. Sometimes the best service you can provide to this person is to refer him to a different opportunity.

The direct result of mutual aid? Agencies benefit by building a mixed volunteer core and expanding their own power base. If you help another organization at one time, it — or its volunteers — may come to your rescue someday. Take the first Rocky Mountain Book Festival in Denver. The majority of its need for volunteers was short-term (three or four days) and unskilled, fairly simple in terms of recruitment. However, the numbers of people required was enormous for a first-time event that had virtually no volunteer base of its own.

The Denver Public Library directed the recruitment and placement effort, drawing from a variety of businesses and organizations that were involved. Many of our short-term or event volunteers assisted at the activity, providing them with an additional positive interaction on behalf of the library. In turn, we discovered a significant quantity of new people who were interested in increasing their involvement with book-related projects.

So keep that rolodex handy as a means of networking and sharing volunteers. Categories best suited for referrals are seasonal volunteers (those who work a special event like an annual book sale) or specialized volunteers with hard-to-locate skills such as graphic design, oral storytelling, or training. Last is the person you just can't use yourself because of time or location constraints or the individual's personal interests.

The volunteer manager must get to know as many people in the volunteer community as possible to make cross-referrals successful. The networks you establish for recruitment, support, and outreach pay off here, too. Other agencies learn that you will assist them and that you can be relied upon to treat people they refer well.

CORPORATE PARTNERSHIPS

The key to a formal partnership with a corporation is to discover a natural link between particular corporate and nonprofit missions and to build a relationship that is both long-term and multifaceted.

Remember corporate partnerships are relatively untapped resources for libraries. You'll be breaking new ground, and this may take time and determination. Businesses are accustomed to appeals from United Way or local health-care organizations, but not libraries.

Relationships that help a business and a nonprofit group meet their needs, fall into at least one of these areas:

- In-kind donations
- Employee volunteer programs
- Sponsorships
- Sponsored advertisements
- Cause-related marketing

A good partnership is distinguished by the corporation's commitment to a cause over time AND the library's flexibility in developing schedules and activities that meet corporate needs. Models in this area are businesses that regularly sponsor charity runs or concerts, restaurants which annually cater a benefit ball, and the yearly drive for holiday toys at a telephone company.

ADDRESS A "COMMON CAUSE"

Any major collaboration—joint fund-raiser, political campaign, large special event—needs a plan to increase its potential for success. Keep these elements in mind when creating your team:

1. Look at how each group's mission will benefit the whole. Find the fit—common needs, common goals, common activities. You're a library; a business might have a commitment to literacy. You serve children with your summer reading program; the local parks department does the same with crafts.

2. Testimonials help build commitment to the effort. Once a displaced homemaker, a library staffer who received vocational training courtesy of a service group now becomes an active promoter of its job search workshop in the library.

3. Draw on everyone's strengths, know everyone's weaknesses. You'll realize just exactly what each agency can contribute to the effort. You may have the most experience preparing long-range schedules while another agency might be able to ask a graphic designer to produce a brochure.

4. Try to make your mutual aid society exciting and fun. Working toward a common goal shouldn't be drudgery, and part of the pleasure of a team is being a member and working together. If you can't laugh together over a cup of coffee, you probably won't be able to show a united front on minimum funding levels.

5. Know the limits of your organization. Are you willing to contribute a quarter of your time to the common cause or an hour or two a month? Sacrifice autonomy on a political issue? Maybe your library or local government places restrictions on your involvement. No one can plan adequately without a reality base.

6. Emphasize good, clear communication. If misunderstandings or disagreements arise, resolve them right away. This should be based on the understanding that achieving the goal together is more important than conforming to some dictatorial method advocated by one person. ("There's more than one way to skin a cat!")

7. Write contracts, detail agreements. These do more to eliminate disagreements and poor communication than all the good will in the world. Record methodology and statistics so you can replicate the good parts, reduce the less-successful. Once the activity is completed, don't forget to evaluate results so you can tell what you've achieved.

8. Toot your own horn about your success. Truth to tell, people like a winner more than an underdog IF they can become part of the triumph. They can't do that unless they know about your efforts. Pat yourselves on the back, too, with a celebration at the completion of a project.

Now that you have a pool of volunteers, what do you do with them? The next chapter gets you started.

3 FOUNDATION

ORGANIZATIONAL STRUCTURE

The position of the volunteer program in the management structure indicates the relative importance of volunteers to a library, how the program functions with and for other positions, and who reports to whom. For those institutions which formalize their management of volunteers, two models exist—consolidated or disbursed.

CONSOLIDATED MANAGEMENT OF VOLUNTEERS

One person, the director, is responsible for the entire volunteer program. She may consult with others but by and large she recruits, orients, trains, places, evaluates, and recognizes all volunteers. He may be head of the library or a staff member selected especially for the responsibility. Supervision of the program and volunteers occurs in the same manner as that of paid staff.

If your institution is small, with no more than two facilities, you may find this method most efficient. By consolidating all functions, the need for record-keeping and communication is minimized.

Some larger library systems use a consolidated model by enabling separate branches or offices to run separate volunteer programs. While each site gains autonomy and immediate localized responsibility, confusion and inconsistency also may result. Recruitment is difficult, and differences in procedures may lead to disagreements among both staff members and volunteers. If your library operates in this manner, you'll have to make inter-agency communication a high priority.

DISBURSED MANAGEMENT OF VOLUNTEERS

The consolidated model proves unwieldy for medium to large libraries where the number and complexity of tasks proliferate. It also does not take advantage of the resources of the total staff.

In the disbursed system, a director/manager oversees the entire effort, but all staff have some part in the supervision of volunteers in their particular units. The director recruits and screens applicants, matches them to the most appropriate jobs, provides initial orientation, and then deploys them to whichever units need assistance. Day-to-day supervision of most volunteers becomes part of the line staff's jobs because the volunteers are integral to delivery of services. Some volunteers work under the direct supervision of the volunteer office, but the majority are placed throughout the library in a disbursed approach.

Each component of the library shows its support for and commitment to the volunteer program by utilizing volunteers. Because most staff members work with volunteers, each person wins when the volunteer program is successful.

LEADING THE WAY

The single most critical component of a volunteer program is its leader. Whether the title is manager, director, coordinator, or supervisor, the position must be part of the professional staff—the peer of librarians and other specialists. He or she must have the authority to make the full range of administrative decisions; he or she must exhibit the ability to lead coupled with a vision for the volunteer program and the institution.

Ideally, the director of volunteers holds a full-time position, assisted by direct support staff if possible. In any case, the lines of duty, the exact responsibilities should be kept as clear and distinct as possible from other duties and occupy as high a priority as they.

BACKGROUND AND SKILLS

What type of background and skills make a good director of volunteers? A college degree, experience within a library, and broad-based community contacts. Also preferable—a history with volunteerism, both as a volunteer and managing volunteers.

Less measurable is the ability to simultaneously lead, or set direction and to let go. After all, what is the purpose of a volunteer program? To permit, even encourage, staff and volunteers to exercise their judgment, take responsibility, and function well together as a team. In addition, the director should be able to create a vision for the volunteer program that inspires people.

Other skills include the following:

1. Ability to relate to, work with, and direct the activities of diverse people from all backgrounds and ages.
2. Experience creating, tracking, and living within budgets. Fund–raising is also very helpful.
3. Good written and verbal communication.
4. Management capabilities to establish and maintain office goals, objectives, record-keeping, and evaluations.

The director of volunteers may have a personality somewhat different from that of other library employees. Remember, this individual's primary function is managing people, not locating information. Furthermore, he manages people who work for the agency only because they choose to. Locating the person who will organize your program may require an uncommon search and selection process for your library.

VOLUNTEER PROGRAM COMPONENTS

Volunteer programs vary according to the size, location, and priorities of libraries. But all professionally managed efforts share certain basic components as follows:

1. The volunteer program maintains an appropriate quantity of written procedures and job descriptions to provide guidance to all involved. These are reviewed and updated as needed.
2. A staff member has responsibility for maintaining written records of individual volunteers, assignments, evaluations, and related matters, with regard for confidentiality and legalities.
3. Recruits receive introductory material in a timely manner, and then are interviewed and either assigned or deferred promptly.
4. Recruits interview with staff to see if the library's needs dovetail with the potential volunteers' skills and wishes. Volunteers and staff mutually agree on assignments.
5. Volunteers receive adequate training to fulfill their duties.
6. Volunteers and staff gain formal and informal recognition for their efforts.

JOB DESIGN

You have a dozen unfinished tasks that you put off from day to day, or week to week. You have a hundred ideas that you've never had time to try. How do you decide which, if any, of these is appropriate as a job for a volunteer? First, the job should be meaningful, valuable to the library and its customers, and not made-up work simply to fill time. It should support the goals and policies of the library, have specific duties, a definable structure, and a staff supervisor.

On the other hand, it should not replace the duties of a paid employee (volunteers are a bonus, not a way to reduce expenses!). It should be structured to meet the needs, skills, and schedules of appropriate potential volunteers and provide a sense of satisfaction and group affiliation. Ideally the job should contain challenges and learning opportunities, and lead to a "career ladder" of new responsibilities if desired.

Now flip the picture around and consider it from the library's point of view. Is the work cost-effective when performed by a volunteer, or will you expend a disproportionate amount of energy and money developing the job? Of course, you must have support systems and policies in place and staff willing to work with volunteers.

JOB DESCRIPTIONS

Why is a job description for volunteers necessary? A prevailing attitude exists that they should just get out there and do the work they are assigned. Job descriptions for volunteers clarify roles and responsibilities; they are as essential as job descriptions for paid employees, who tend to develop on their own through spoken or unspoken consent even if the job descriptions are not written down.

Suppose a volunteer committee is considering the planning of a storytelling festival. Because of our familiarity with parliamentary procedure, we expect the chairman to direct us, make assignments of duties, and check on follow-through. We expect a committee member to accept or reject a task depending upon time, interest, and skills. One might offer to contact storytellers or spontaneously suggest forming a subcommittee to do so. Another might prefer to remain in the background but provide support by writing letters.

These individuals, by following their natural preferences, are defining their jobs. By and large they know (or can work out) what they are to do. Likewise, a jack-of-all-trades stationed at a branch library every Friday for ten years needs little description of his duties.

But what if this person suddenly moves? Can you fill the gap, lacking knowledge of his duties? And if a disagreement arises on the storytelling committee about who should have done what, how can that be resolved? The advantages of written descriptions for your volunteers are threefold:

1. They provide a recruitment tool by defining responsibilities that enable a potential volunteer to decide if his skills and interests match.

2. They detail the training or skill level required to complete the job successfully, thus assisting the director and staff supervisors to supervise adequately.

3. They provide a basis for evaluation along with subsequent recognition or reassignment of volunteers. The director of volunteers uses job descriptions in the initial interview as a screening device. Those who do not meet the job's criteria can be redirected with no bad feelings.

On a very practical level, job descriptions provide solid help across the board to library employees from the director of volunteers by establishing expectations. This helps produce a productive, well-adjusted team of staff and volunteers.

Who creates job descriptions? Anyone with the inclination if possible. Certainly staff members who will be working with the assigned volunteers should be involved. Volunteers themselves can provide valuable insight. However the director of volunteers has ultimate responsibility.

What goes into a job description? *Who, what, where, when, why, how* are good beginning points. You want to provide enough information to tempt potential volunteers with the position's attractive points while simultaneously conveying a realistic view of the time and location requirements and desirable skills. These can include the following:

- Job title,
- Function: need for the job, its purpose to the library,
- General statement of duties,
- Examples of duties,
- Supervision exercised, supervisor,
- Qualifications,
- Time frame: Approximate number of hours by day, week, or month as well as number of months' commitment,
- Location of the job, and
- Benefits and opportunities.

Regardless how appealing or well-written a job description may be, it is useless if no one fills the position. The approach to volunteers' job descriptions should be flexible enough to permit rewriting and adaptation to fit each situation's uniqueness. See the following sample job descriptions for a homebound services coordinator, homebound volunteer, volunteer staff aide, and a special projects volunteer provided in Figures 3-1, 3-2, 3-3, and 3-4.

FIGURE 3-1: Job Description—Homebound Services Coordinator

General Statement of Duties:	• Coordinates volunteers for the homebound program. Works under the direct supervision of volunteer services manager. • Promotes a positive public image of the public library through all contacts with individuals and groups. • Works to ascertain homebound needs in the community.
Examples of Duties:	• Plans effective use of homebound volunteers. • Matches volunteers with homebound customers according to geographic location. • Works with volunteer services manager to develop training needs; assists with homebound volunteer recognition; evaluates homebound program and volunteers; acts as liaison between customer and staff. • Uses knowledge of appropriate library staff/volunteers in selecting materials for homebound customers. • Maintains accurate records.
Supervises:	Supervises homebound volunteers.
Location:	At home or office; flexibility to meet with volunteer services manager and volunteers at selected sites.
Qualifications:	• Knowledge of management practices and methods necessary to administer homebound program. • Working knowledge of community. • Skills in recruiting, scheduling, training and record keeping. • Ability to plan and determine homebound volunteer requirements. • Ability to use productive and sensitive interpersonal and intergroup relationship skills.
Time frame:	Contracts for one year of service.
Supervisor:	Volunteer services manager.

FIGURE 3-2: Job Description—Homebound Volunteer

General Statement of Duties:	• Delivers library materials to homebound customers, under the direction of the volunteer services manager and homebound coordinator. • Promotes a positive public image of the Public Library through all contacts with homebound customer.
Examples of Duties:	• Assists homebound customer with selection of reading material from the library's collection through the use of large print books catalog, books-on-tape list, etc. • Helps homebound customer to complete library card application if needed. • Discusses reading preference with customer. • Returns materials to library when due and/or when customer is finished.
Supervises:	None.
Location:	• Variety of branches and homebound customer's residence.
Qualifications:	• Complete volunteer skillsbank. • Receive and review homebound training packet. • Ability to work effectively with a diverse public and staff. • Complete Criminal Bureau of Investigation (CBI) check. • Access to transportation as needed.
Time frame:	Work a minimum of three hours every six weeks. Commit to six months of service.
Supervisor:	Volunteer services manager or homebound service coordinator.

FIGURE 3-3: Job Description—Volunteer Staff Aide

General Statement of Duties:	• Assists staff members with clerical tasks, basic research, circulation activities, computer and audio-visual usage, and materials repair. • Promotes a positive public image of the Public Library through all contacts with library staff and customers.
Examples of Duties:	• Helps with typing, word processing, photocopying, alphabetizing, filing, shelf reading, and other general clerical projects. • Handles books, and other library materials. • Telephones customers with book notices.
Supervises:	None.
Qualifications:	• Basic clerical skills, willingness to help and to learn new skills, openness to new ideas and experiences. • Ability to work effectively with a diverse public and staff.
Time frame:	Works a minimum of two hours per week. Contracts for three months of services.
Location:	Branches as needed.
Supervisor:	Volunteer services manager, senior clerk, or other library staff as designated.

FIGURE 3-4: Job Description—Special Projects Volunteer

General Statement of Duties:	• Assists with displays, archives, graphics, oral histories, community festivals, book-sorting, speakers bureau, read-aloud, special collections, and community outreach. • Promotes a positive public image of the Public Library through all contacts with library staff and customers. • Takes training necessary to perform duties of special projects (e.g., read-aloud training, speaker's bureau training).
Examples of Duties:	• Reads aloud to pre-school children. • Gathers archival materials. • Conducts oral histories. • Works information booth at special community events. • Speaks to community groups (e.g., book talk groups). • Works annual Friends Book Sale. • Works with library staff to create, develop, and exhibit special displays in branch libraries and at Central Library.
Supervises:	None.
Location:	Varies; selected branches, special events sites.
Qualifications:	• Completed volunteer skillsbank. • Demonstrated special skills in area of specialty by bringing examples of work (e.g., portfolios, etc.). • Ability to work effectively with a diverse public and staff.
Time frame:	Works a minimum of four hours per week or duration of special project.
Supervisor:	Volunteer services manager, special project manager

JOB REVIEWS

Review job descriptions periodically, compare to individual performance, and consider changes. A review provides continuing satisfaction for the volunteer and greater performance for your agency. You can adapt the position slightly or make major changes to encourage the volunteer's growth. Would any of these points improve some tired old positions at your library?

1. **Enhancement:** Delegate management or supervisory responsibilities and authority.
2. **Sequence:** Add steps in a series to reach a goal rather than repeating the same task over and over.
3. **Reduction:** Abolish useless or duplicative tasks even if "we've always done it this way."
4. **Expansion:** Increase the number and diversity of tasks assigned to a particular position.
5. **Combination:** Combine or rotate tedious or repetitive actions.
6. **Career ladders:** Develop a progression of jobs that build upon one another, through which a volunteer can be "promoted" by demonstrating skill and experience.

PROCEDURES AND MANUALS

Procedures and manuals are essential for achieving consistency and continuity, which are the instruments for building good relations between paid and unpaid staff. For staff members, procedures summarize information about volunteers and how to place, evaluate, and manage them. Manuals delineate reasonable functions and responsibilities for the Volunteer Office, staff, and volunteers, and describe their interactions.

Volunteers can also derive benefit. Procedures assist the volunteer by giving a written record of regular and special operations of the department, background on the agency, organizational chart, mission statement, procedures for illness or leave, and other pertinent information. These often are contained in an orientation packet or volunteer handbook and may also be distributed over time as they are developed, or to volunteers functioning in certain capacities—for example, story readers.

Written procedures frequently develop organically, following habit or custom. Sometimes they precede a project or situation. In any case, to be effective, they need to meet four criteria:

- Keep them simple; the fewer and the shorter, the better.
- Gain agreement about procedures from all staff who may be affected. They could even write draft rules for you.
- Be flexible. Procedures should not be so rigorous that they destroy individual initiative or enjoyment in the job.
- Review procedures periodically to make sure they retain their practicality and effectiveness. Once every year or two is not too often.

Your procedures should be those that impact the volunteer-agency relationship. You needn't include other procedures—for example, rules for shelving materials or telephone answering techniques—that have to do with library operations themselves. Components of procedures might include the following:

- Definition of volunteers,
- Role of the Volunteer Office,
- A statement about utilization of volunteers and scope of the program,
- An overview of processes including job descriptions, recruitment, screening and placement, interviews, orientation, training, record-keeping,
- Volunteer benefits and recognition,
- Volunteer rights and responsibilities,
- Limitation of liability for risk and personal injury,
- Evaluation techniques,
- Process for counseling or mediation to solve concerns,
- Procedures for illness, resignation, termination, leave,
- Procedures for volunteers with special status such as community service placements or those with disabilities, and
- Sample forms.

4 ASSESSMENT AND PLACEMENT

The day has come when a potential volunteer has made contact with you. What are the steps you take to move from interest into placement? The sequence can be compressed into a single meeting, but it usually develops as follows:

- Conduct initial screening—probably by telephone, maybe in person at an event or in your office.
- Evaluate recruitment response—How did the individual learn about the library's needs?
- Furnish general volunteer opportunity flyer, job bulletin or job descriptions, and skills form (see Figure 4-1).
- Receive completed skills form.
- Schedule and conduct personal interview.
- Place the volunteer.

This sequence is most useful for regular, longer-term volunteers. Volunteers that are serving at events or for a one-shot session are best and most quickly screened by detailing the times and duties and letting the people self-select.

SCREENING VOLUNTEERS

Effective screening improves program quality by matching volunteers with the best assignment. It helps to eliminate unsuitable applicants without a trial period through which the volunteer and the staff struggle. Screening is not a substitute for *intuition*. Body language, informal conversation are all small indicators which provide additional, if unquantifiable, information about preferences and skills. Use your intuition to ask more questions.

Multiple surveys increase your chance of finding the best volunteers. The following guidelines will help you screen recruits:

- Use a written description to indicate to the recruit the required skills and guide the supervisor's responsibilities.
- Before you assign a position, collect all pertinent information—availability, preferences, skills, and references.
- Be sensitive to cultural and personality differences. Remember, the goal is to recruit the best individual for a position, not a new best friend.
- Pose important concerns in a variety of ways so that the person being recruited gives well-rounded information.

- Complete security check when the job requires it.
- Include others in the screening process. The recruit will work with people in a singular situation, and someone else may pick up signals that you miss.
- However, not all positions require long-term commitment or a high level of responsibility. Be flexible; you don't need the third degree for all recruits.
- Don't waste time searching for irrelevant facts and details. Do you care if a volunteer shelver has children? No, but the point may be pertinent with a storyteller.
- Be consistent. If the position requires a background check, require the check from all volunteers performing the same task.

SECURITY CLEARANCES

Criminal background checks eliminate known offenders and convicted criminals. People with dubious incentives think twice before applying when they know that you'll be reviewing their records.

Clearances are especially critical when volunteers deal autonomously with vulnerable populations—the elderly, persons with disabilities, minors—or handle major financial transactions. At the Denver Public Library, people involved with Services to the Homebound receive this screening specialty because they visit the elderly and people with physical disabilities under their own direct supervision.

If you're not sure which avenues are available to you, check with your local police department, state criminal investigation bureau, or city attorney. They can enlighten you on what you are *required* to do, along with what you *can* do.

When you are dealing with security matters, screening procedures may seem daunting. But keep your priorities focused on protecting your customers and fulfilling your mission. Institute additional safeguards into your program—for example, thorough ongoing management, specific training of volunteers and supervisors, and periodic evaluations.

This series of activities is a continuation of recruitment and the initiation of training. It can be done over the telephone or in person. The primary purpose of screening and interviewing is to see if the volunteer and the agency "match." Does the library have projects and activities that can benefit from this particular volunteer's assistance? Does the individual have the skills, the interest, and the time to fill a volunteer role?

THE PERSONAL INTERVIEW

When you have received the skills form (or a substitute, such as a resumé and letter), you need to conduct an interview in person or by telephone. As you discuss these topics with the volunteer, you can expand on information to increase the chances of a successful placement. Depending upon time and location, you can use the following questions at the first interview or at a later date to obtain a personality sketch of the potential volunteer.

1. Where have you volunteered previously? What did you do?
2. Why did you leave?
3. What did you like about volunteering?
4. Why do you want to volunteer with the library?
5. What kind of experience are you seeking from us?
6. Tell me about your abilities.
7. What would you like to improve about yourself?
8. Do you enjoy working with people? Give an example.
9. How can you help the work of our library?

Unfortunately, you may not have the time or the inclination to go into this depth with every individual. Some people let you know right from the beginning exactly what activities interest them. One young mother attending a library function mentioned to a staff member that she was seeking volunteer work that would enable her to keep up her writing skills and work at home. Another retired man contacted the office in response to a specific article in the newspaper requesting researchers.

However, if the volunteer position requires a certain set of skills or personality, or if the individual is proving a challenge to place, Figure 4-1 is designed to help you select the proper fit. Each sentence is finished by the potential volunteer, and you should encourage examples and discussion.

1. During my free time, I . . .
2. The biggest challenge I have encountered is. . .
3. The job I liked best was. . .
4. My greatest worry is. . .
5. If I could have any job in the world it would be. . .
6. You can predict things will fail if. . .
7. The activity or work I'll avoid if I can is. . .
8. The boss I like best is. . .
9. Something that ticks me off is. . .
10. I am most proud of. . . .

INTERVIEWING TECHNIQUES

Do you freeze when you conduct an interview? Feel like a judge? Never get quite the information you need? Ten tips are listed to see what fits your style.

1. The setting of the interview should be welcoming and not intimidating; a special place where you can focus all your attention on the interview. Clear your calendar so you don't need to rush; and hold your calls.

2. Small points make a big difference. Watch your body language; use the interviewee's first name in conversation.

3. Offer a refreshment, a cup of coffee, if possible.

4. Be specific about your role as the volunteer director; about what you and your library are prepared to do or provide.

5. The more precise the response, the easier the placement. Ask the recruit to clarify and give examples about vague points.

6. Avoid personal comments; just be a good listener. You are talking to a potential volunteer, not a new friend. Above all, don't argue or debate. This is a difficult task at times, especially when the recruit may be making personal comments to you!

7. Avoid leading questions or statements that might influence an answer or decision, such as "Don't you think . . . ?".

8. You are neither judge nor confessor. Eliminate comments that appear to evaluate an individual's opinion or background. Stress the confidentiality of your process. This is particularly important when you are dealing with court-placed volunteers.

9. The more you talk, the less you are listening. Although you should be able to direct the interview—some folks never end their narrative about personal experiences unless you establish limits—the recruit should provide most of the conversation.

10. Know your volunteer program. If you are familiar with the requirements for each position, you'll be more comfortable directing the interview and less likely to wind up being the subject. Above all, relax and enjoy the interview.

MATCHING THE VOLUNTEER TO THE JOB

FILLING A VOLUNTEER'S MANAGEMENT POSITION

Sometimes you are seeking an individual to assume a management position or take on a highly responsible project. Perhaps you are recruiting for the chairmanship of a fund-raising dinner or a book discussion group. In this instance, your interview is more intensive. Pick and choose from these discussion points to gain a sense of the person's abilities:

- Tell me about a time you were responsible for managing a big project or had to manage many other people.
- How do you establish rapport with and gain cooperation from people whose backgrounds are very different from yours?
- Have you ever been a mentor or teacher to encourage someone else's growth?
- What type of supervision do you prefer?
- How would you train or instruct others to use equipment? In new procedures?
- Which gets better results—working alone or with others?
- How do you set priorities in your life? How do you handle conflicts among priorities?
- What rewards do you expect from an activity?
- How do you feel when someone ignores or opposes you?
- When are the right times for you to take the initiative?
- What would the people you work with say about you?

These questions initiate a discussion to help you determine if the match will be good. There is no sense in assigning a rugged individualist who hates close supervision to work with a persnickety woman who absolutely *must* have personal involvement with every step of a project. And regardless of his intelligence, the loner won't enjoy facing the public over a reference desk.

You also need to use your sensitivity and intuition to calculate the fit. Subtle cues like attire, grammar, topics discussed, and general knowledge help you decide if you should recruit this particular person for a highly responsible job.

VOLUNTEER SKILLS FORM

The first line of assessment is the skills form or a similar type of questionnaire. Comparable to a job application, it summarizes the applicant's demographic information and provides a list of skills, or interests, as well as hobbies. Figure 4-1 is an example of a skills form.

Because this form is integral to all placements and records, take time to plan it well. It is particularly valuable if it can be converted to computerized data bases. Then you are able to access groups of volunteers by categories such as skills, interests, or time schedules almost immediately.

You need to include basics like name, address, phone numbers,

FIGURE 4-1: Skillsbank Form

Denver Public Library
Skillsbank

What is a Skillsbank? The Skillsbank is a service which recruits and matches volunteers with library needs. It is a listing of persons who are willing to share their special skills and interests with various library community service groups on a short-term or ongoing basis.

Identify your skills. . .interests. . .hobbies. . .training. . .experiences. Register these valuable resources with the Denver Public Library Volunteer Skillsbank. Involve yourself with various services, programs and projects in community service activities.

Volunteers of all ages, experiences, and locations in the community are needed. Short and long term volunteers are needed. You can specify your own availability and select your assignments. Your skills and interests will be matched appropriately.

CHECK THE CATEGORIES and select those areas related to you. COMPLETE THE FORM on page 3. You will be contacted to discuss your involvement prior to any referrals. Should you have questions about Skillsbank, call 640-8957. TDD information for persons with hearing impairments, 640-8980. Your call will be returned within one week of receipt of this form.

--- VOLUNTEER SKILLS/INTERESTS LIST ---

Circle the appropriate number(s) identifying your areas of interest, skill, or personal hobby that you would be willing to share as a Library volunteer.

0100 **ARTS/GRAPHICS/CRAFTS**	
0101 crafts (general)	
0102 architectural drawing	
0103 art exhibits/fairs	
0104 calligraphy	
0105 cartooning	
0106 commercial art/designing	
0107 exhibit planning	
0108 history	
0109 illustrating	
0110 literature	

0200 **BUSINESS ADMINISTRATION**
0201 computer systems
0202 goal setting
0203 management training
0204 marketing/advertising
0205 public relations
0206 statistics

0300 **CLERICAL/OFFICE WORK**
0301 clerical (general)
0302 bulk mailings
0303 file clerk
0304 receptionist
0305 records clerk
0306 secretary/stenographer
0307 telephoning
0308 typing
0309 word processing

0400 **COMMUNICATIONS/ INFORMATION SYSTEMS**
0401 audio-visual (general)
0402 brochure/newsletter
0403 cable
0404 communications systems
0405 copy writing/editing
0406 film production
0407 film reviewing
0408 information systems
0409 interviewing
0410 journalism/technical writing
0411 photography
0412 printing/typesetting
0413 public speaking
0414 publishing
0415 radio broadcasting
0416 recording
0417 skillsbank systems
0418 sound technician
0419 taping
0420 video tape production
0421 writing (general)

0500 **EDUCATION**
0501 day care/extended day programs
0502 literacy/G.E.D. programs
0503 living history
0504 preschool/headstart programs
0505 primary school education
0506 secondary school education
0507 special education; gifted, handicapped
0508 tutor; English second language

0600 **ENTERTAINMENT**
0601 band instruments
0602 clown/mime
0603 folk singer
0604 guitar
0605 music (general)
0606 puppeteering
0607 song leading
0608 story telling
0609 theater arts
0610 travel

0700 **ENVIRONMENT**
0701 energy conservation
0702 environment/energy
0703 naturalist

0800 **FINANCIAL MANAGEMENT**
0801 financial management (general)
0802 budget plans/preparing
0803 fund raising
0804 grant/proposal writing
0805 program budgeting
0806 tax counseling

FIGURE 4-1: Continued

0900 **HOMEBOUND SERVICES**
0901 reading
0902 showing films
0903 visiting

1000 **LANGUAGES**
1001 Braille
1002 Cambodian
1003 Chinese
1004 English
1005 French
1006 German
1007 Greek
1008 Italian
1009 Korean
1010 Laotian
1011 Russian
1012 Sign Language
1013 Spanish
1014 Vietnamese

1100 **LAW/LAW ENFORCEMENT**
1101 law enforcement (general)
1102 consumer rights
1103 patent/copyright law

1200 **LIBRARY/RESEARCH**
1201 research (general)
1202 archives/manuscripts
1203 bookbinding
1204 cataloging
1205 genealogy
1206 legislative research
1207 librarian
1208 library services
1209 local history
1210 opinion surveying/polling
1211 oral history
1212 paper conservation
1213 rare books
1214 reading/recording for blind
1215 research developing

1300 **MERCHANDISING**
1301 book sale
1302 cashier
1303 gift shop work
1304 sales clerk
1305 sales management

1400 **PUBLIC ADMINISTRATION**
1401 community organizing
1402 conference/workshop planning
1403 project coordinating
1404 program development
1405 urban planning
1406 volunteer program management

1500 **SKILLED TRADES/ CONSTRUCTION**
1501 skilled trades (general)

OTHERS:
(Any skills/interests not listed above)

_____

_____

_____

_____

_____

FIGURE 4-1: Continued

Library Administrative Center
Volunteer Office
1330 Fox St.
Denver, CO 80204-2602
Telephone: 640-8957

VOLUNTEER PROFILE

Library Location _____

PLEASE PRINT AND ANSWER ALL QUESTIONS

Date _____

| Last Name | First Name | Middle Name |

Street Address _____ Telephone (work) _____

City _____ Zip Code _____ Telephone (home) _____

Male_____ Female_____ Colorado Driver's License Number_____

Birthday —— Day | Month

Age Categories: Under 18_____ 18-24_____ 25-39_____ 40-60_____ over 60_____

EDUCATION: (Highest Level) Grammar School_____ High School_____ Technical School_____ Some College_____

College Degree(s) or Professional Training in _____

_____

AVAILABILITY: [ ] Mon. [ ] Tues. [ ] Wed. [ ] Thurs. [ ] Fri. [ ] Sat.

Mornings_____ Afternoons_____ Evenings_____

Hours per week_____ On Call_____ Flexible_____

Of those areas of interest, skill or personal hobby which you circled, please elaborate on your level of experience (training/education, interest only, hobbyist) and the type of involvement you prefer (direct service, consultant, tutor, speaker).

_____

_____

_____

_____

_____

Have you ever been a volunteer for any organization before? Yes_____ No_____

If yes, please specify (include other communities)._____

_____

_____

_____

Would you consider being a member of a Volunteer Board? Yes_____ No_____

By registering with the Skillsbank, you are under no obligation to accept any placement unless you choose to do so. Call 640-8957 for any explanation about the form.

_____

References (other volunteer experiences – church, school, hospital, etc.)

Name _____ Name _____

Address _____ Address _____

Telephone _____ Telephone _____

In case of emergency, contact: _____

_____

Phone: _____

FIGURE 4-1: Continued

VOLUNTEER PROFILE INTERVIEW

Date assigned_____

Supervisor _____

Branch/Department_____

Training Received _____

Interviewer's Comments:

_____

_____

_____

_____

_____

It is a normal part of the Denver Public Library Homebound Volunteer procedure to check on the suitability of new volunteers due to the nature and sensitivity of the work. Successful completion of the criminal check is a qualification to work in the Homebound Volunteer Program at the Denver Public Library.

_____
Applicant's Signature

I authorize Denver Public Library to attain necessary information that pertains only to the requirements for volunteering at DPL as stated from the Denver Police Department.

_____   _____
Name   Date of Birth

_____   _____
Social Security Number   Today's Date

and emergency information. Another portion covers types of tasks or areas of responsibility from which the recruit selects. The final part enables the interviewer to jot down notes during the interview. The form is part of the volunteer's permanent file, which becomes public record. Keep the information up to date in case of emergency or other pressing need.

No document is an absolute necessity. A resume or letter can fill the same functions. But you'll find that use of a skills or application form establishes the importance of volunteering as well as capturing helpful initial information.

Make sure you point out any legal requirements from your library's perspective. For example, if you're going to be performing a check of criminal records, you must let the applicant know and obtain his signature as a release.

REQUESTING VOLUNTEERS

To expedite the allocation of volunteers, you can depend on telephone calls or casual remarks from various branches and offices. Or you can ask for requests in writing. Formal documents enable you to centralize all current openings at your fingertips. They also provide a paper trail for record-keeping and statistical analysis.

The requests for volunteers are used in conjunction with job descriptions. They provide the specifics for each position. Figure 4-2 is an example of a "Request for Volunteers" form.

PRESENTING OPPORTUNITIES

Beyond the list of qualifications or interests lie motivators for recruits. As discussed in Chapter 3, Foundation, people volunteer for a number of reasons. Although some people can tell you immediately that they are volunteering to make new friends or learn computer skills, sometimes you must make an educated guess.

In the course of your screening, the applicant may ask questions or make comments that will assist you in your placement of them. He or she may wonder if he will have other people that can be assigned to parts of a large project. This is an indication of "management" potential. As you gain a sense of the individual's needs, you can compare volunteer opportunities. You can weigh options for social interaction, recognition, challenge, mental stimulation, or service.

Sift through job descriptions and requests for volunteers to select one or more that may appeal to the recruit. Even if that person has a specific position in mind, you might want to present others that are high priority for filling or that suit her qualifications.

FIGURE 4-2: Request For Volunteers

REQUEST FOR VOLUNTEERS

Date of Request:_____

Branch/Department:_____
Position:_____
Duties: _____

_____

_____

Time Commitment: Hours/Days _____ Duration:_____

Requested starting date:_____

Qualifications or Special Skills(including age requirements):
  ex.: Typing, Computer Skills, Filing, Art/Crafts, Read Aloud, other:(be specific)

_____

_____

Special Job Considerations: (ex. lifting, long term, standing, etc.)

_____

_____

Supervision by:_____Phone:_____

_____
Department/Branch Manager   Date
****
VOLUNTEER SERVICES OFFICE USE ONLY:
Date Received:_____

Name (s) of volunteer(s)   Date skillsbank sent   Action taken
_____
_____
_____
_____

*Action taken:
  Filled /date: _____

  Referred/date_____
  On hold/date_____

When you have a tentative match between the individual and the job, refer the volunteer to the staff member who will be making the final placement. It usually is more appropriate to rely on the staff member to schedule an appointment with the volunteer. However, if time is critical—for example, with community service personnel—or the employee has been unable to contact the volunteer, you can ask the volunteer to initiate the interview.

FOLLOW UP

Touch base with the volunteer after a few weeks to check whether the volunteer and the supervisor have met. Has a placement occurred? Or do you need to offer an alternative?

Again you need to put into play all of your intuition, because the volunteer or staff member may not be able to articulate a particular concern. For example, a self-described "self-starter" was eager to use computers. However, it quickly became apparent that this person couldn't read the fine print on the screen and lacked the experience and the innate talent to perform the tasks. Without intervention by the supervisor and discussions with the volunteer director, this volunteer would have quietly faded away from the library, a sense of frustration and failure his only results. Instead he was reassigned to a position that related to his needs.

Critical for the well-being of all staff and volunteers is a sense of security to say "no." If the "fit" feels wrong, if the position has changed, or the personalities don't mesh, that's fine. Far better for you, the library, and the volunteer, when you make an alternative suggestion.

What if nothing appeals to the recruit, and you can't place him? Let him know as soon as you can, along with your plans for the future. Is something else coming up soon? Would you like to keep the application on file? Refer the recruit to another agency? You can also perform a service by notifying library staff of the availability of recruits with particular skills and schedules.

FORMALIZING A VOLUNTEER—AGENCY RELATIONSHIP

The formalization of the volunteer-agency relationship is becoming accepted. Why make a formal agreement that can't be enforced? Some people feel that a written form helps to establish standards and encourages compliance with various requirements, including scheduling. The document carries an insinuation of the ethical weight of a pledge or contract. It underscores the value of the volunteer's services to the library. However, no one can be forced to sign an agreement. If your library decides to require such a registration, you may find recruits who object and choose not to volunteer. Figure 4-3 is a sample agreement.

FIGURE 4-3: Library/Volunteer Agreement Courtesy of Indianapolis—Marion County Public Library

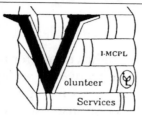

LIBRARY/VOLUNTEER AGREEMENT

This agreement is intended to indicate the seriousness with which we treat our volunteers. The intent of the agreement is to assure you both of our deep appreciation of your services and to indicate our commitment to do the very best we can to make your volunteer experience here a productive and rewarding one.

I.   LIBRARY

We, Indianapolis-Marion County Public Library, agree to accept the services of _____ beginning _____ and we commit to the following:

1.   To provide adequate information, training, and assistance for the volunteer to be able to meet the responsibilities of their position.

2.   To ensure diligent supervisory aid to the volunteer and to provide feedback on performance.

3.   To respect the skills, dignity and individual needs of the volunteer, and to do our best to adjust to these individual requirements.

4.   To treat the volunteer as an equal partner with library staff, jointly responsible for completion of the Library's mission.

II. VOLUNTEER

I, _____, agree to serve as a volunteer for Indianapolis-Marion County Public Library and commit to the following:

1.   To perform my volunteer duties to the best of my ability.

2.   To adhere to Library rules and procedures.

3.   To meet time and duty commitments, or to provide adequate notice so that alternate arrangements can be made.

III. AGREED TO:

_____   _____
Volunteer   Manager, Volunteer Services

_____   _____
Date   Date

When might you prefer to use an agreement? The procedure is especially effective for situations in which you might be asked to validate a person's participation such as an internship or employer-sponsored volunteer time. It also can assist if you experience problems with a particular individual or have difficulty enforcing certain standards.

For example consider this hypothetical situation. A school library depends heavily on volunteers to staff its circulation desk. However, young mothers, who form the volunteer pool, consistently forget to call when they'll be absent. By instituting a new operation with signed agreements, the media specialist ensures that all volunteers are familiar with requirements and take them seriously. When the policy is formalized on paper the volunteers in turn take the guidelines more seriously. This step will help reduce absenteeism.

THE ULTIMATE GOAL

Good recruitment techniques all come down to knowing what you're not going to provide, what you can't provide, as well as the opposite. Not every potential volunteer will be right for your library. Neither the potential volunteer nor the interviewer should feel a sense of failure if you discover the individual's and the library's needs don't fit. Both of you are better off realizing this before time and energy have been invested in training and placement.

Certainly your ability as a director of volunteers does not rest with matching every individual with a position. If the conclusion of an interview is "good-bye and good luck," you needn't take this as a personal failure.

The management of volunteers requires flexibility and creativity in situations where rules frequently don't apply. Your ultimate goal is a contented volunteer who is able to make full use of his skills with confidence while contributing to the well-being of the library.

5 ORIENTATION AND TRAINING

For a volunteer, a new situation can bring a trace of trepidation as well as excitement and enthusiasm. Through orientation and training, you hope to relieve the trepidation, create a productive work setting, and begin building a sense of camaraderie as quickly as possible.

Orientation and training are not the exclusive activities of volunteers. Equally crucial to the success of the volunteer program is the involvement of staff, sometimes as mentor, sometimes as student, and sometimes as cheerleader.

ORIENTATION

A personal orientation makes the volunteer comfortable and knowledgeable about your agency. Depending upon the size of your library system and the complexity of the volunteer program, an orientation may consist of two or three engagements.

In a large agency, the volunteer director often provides the initial orientation, either for individuals or in a group session. Topics include items that all volunteers should know—library history, management structure, and so on.

The second session can be with an agency or department manager. Operating procedures, agreement on tasks and schedule, and supervision are some elements that should be covered. A third session may be conducted by immediate supervisor or co-worker for a tour and precise explanations of the institution's procedures.

Regardless of the number or length of orientations, the final package should include certain essential components.

- A brief overview of the library. Explain the library's mission, goals, role in the community, and vision and value statement.
- The organization of the library and your department. Use an organization chart if there is one to clarify relationships and the chain of command. Explain how branches and departments relate, affect, and work with the other.
- Funding sources, including supporting organizations such as Friends groups that contribute to funding and their role.
- Printed information with policies and procedures.

- A tour of the agency is essential for an individual's comfort level. Assign an area for the volunteer's belongings—hat, coat, briefcase, purse—show location of files or equipment, volunteer records, supplies.
- The volunteer position, your expectations, pertinent policies (such as confidentiality), the chain of command, and specific work.
- A review of necessary forms such as registration documents, job descriptions, evaluations, and any other information data.
- Details about regular staff meetings, conferences, and evaluations and their importance.
- A discussion about the volunteer's expectations, skills, requirements, goals, and preferred work style. Agree on schedule, length of commitment, and tasks. Have the volunteer sign the agreement if he hasn't done so yet.
- Standard operating procedures such as safety rules, sign-in sheets, plans for lunch and coffee breaks. Be especially clear about the volunteer's immediate supervisor, any other people in the chain of command, and who can help the volunteer set priorities.
- Volunteer benefits are an important recruitment tool. Address the benefits that your library offers, and be clear if certain benefits involve fulfillment of particular requirements. For example, a volunteer may need to be on the job for six months before becoming eligible for training classes.
- Introduce the volunteer to the staff. You can assign a staff member or experienced volunteer as a partner to facilitate the initiation period and encourage good relationships.
- Promote the asking of questions and answers. A safe environment is one in which a volunteer can question, learn, even make an occasional mistake without feeling threatened.

Invite the staff to be part of the orientation. They can help create it and accompany the volunteer on a tour or present parts of the activity. A checklist for orientations is provided in Figure 5-1.

THE IMPACT ON AND OF STAFF

The staff's relations with and attitude toward volunteers are absolutely critical to the success or failure of a volunteer program. Every other component can be perfect—a personable and organized volunteer director, the support of management, an adequate bud-

---

FIGURE 5-1: Volunteer Orientation Checklist

____ Mission and goals of library

____ Administrative structure

____ Funding sources

____ Skills bank form/application

____ Volunteer job descriptions

____ Tour of agency

____ Out-of-pocket expenses

____ Safety/parking

____ Coffee, lunch, breaks

____ Office equipment

____ Personal belongings

____ Procedures and policies

____ Forms

____ Future training

____ Benefits

____ Evaluations

____ Meetings, conferences

____ Introductions

____ Questions and answers

---

get, interesting projects — but if staff members are belligerent, or simply indifferent, they can alienate a volunteer immediately.

At a minimum, all staff should extend the same courtesies and support to volunteers that they do to fellow employees. Does this seem like an obvious standard? Not necessarily. In some libraries, volunteers are relegated to second-class status, denied reasonable access to adequate supplies and equipment, ignored when they begin their work, or scolded like children for their errors. No wonder they quickly desert their posts, thus fulfilling the self-fulfilling prophecy made at these agencies, *"Volunteers are unreliable!"* Fortunately, this type of situation is rare.

More frequent and difficult to identify is when a subtle type of bias may be in effect. Volunteers who have been around for a long time or who are friends of employees form an unconscious clique with employees. This type of interaction forms a circle that excludes newcomers or those who appear "different." A person must be very determined to break into this group.

The following list provides you with some examples of how you can reduce the possibility of these types of situations from occurring.

1. Orientation packets and every employee's training and updates should include information about the company's volunteer program. A few sentences can summarize the role of your office and outline the basics about working with volunteers. If possible, add "work with volunteers" to all employees' job descriptions.

2. Work with managers and directors to establish reasonable expectations for interaction and behavior with volunteers, and then put these into effect. Some are ideas identifying a primary contact for volunteers in each branch, familiarizing employees with forms, and supporting recognition of volunteers' efforts. To ensure that expectations are met, top managers must support the effort by *meeting expectations and modeling appropriate behavior themselves.*

3. Involve employees in regular or special projects like drafting job descriptions, planning recognition activities, and developing orientation and training materials. Not only will their involvement give them a stake in the excellence of the volunteer program, but their perspective and opinions also will improve every project they touch.

4. Provide training for staff, especially staff supervisors of volunteers. Not every employee is interested in or suited for supervising volunteers. A combination of native inclination, actual job assignment, and training helps to develop a corps of personnel qualified to work with volunteers. However, basic tenets should be included in the training of all managers, even if they don't directly supervise volunteers. Your objective with all training is to encourage a symbiotic sense of place and teamwork for volunteers and staff.

5. Establish procedures for feedback, evaluations, complaints, and troubleshooting, and implement them with *sensitivity!* Many problems can be eliminated before they start by developing management systems in advance. Certainly staff needs to be assured that they never have to accept an unacceptable volunteer and that the Volunteer Office will handle delicate situations for them. (An example? A male volunteer with roving hands.) Personal contact between you and other staff members is the best way to receive spontaneous suggestions—telephone, visits, and so forth.

6. Delineate the benefits from volunteers and convey these in meetings, training sessions, and support materials. Properly uti-

lized volunteers help with work. They also bring an influx of fresh ideas, and the excitement of new personalities and work styles. They offer the possibility of extra time for staff to try different approaches or new projects. The entire library provides better service, and individuals gain a better work environment.

7. Emphasize supplemental skills staff gained by working with and managing people and projects. In some libraries, supervision of volunteers augments an employee's annual evaluation for salary increases or promotions.

8. Nullify misconceptions about volunteers. Here are some common ones:

- Paid employees will lose their jobs to volunteers.
- Volunteers aren't professional in their approach.
- You can't get rid of poor volunteers.
- Volunteers take more time and energy than they're worth.

Clear policies and guidelines, explicit standards and expectations, involvement of staff, and regular evaluations all will assure staff that they benefit from using volunteers.

BENEFITS TO VOLUNTEERS

The greatest reward any worker—volunteer or paid staff—can receive is satisfaction in doing the work. As volunteers for a library, people gain a broader knowledge of library services and valuable work experience applicable to employment. But additional benefits can make your library a more attractive site for volunteers. Try to brainstorm benefits that volunteers might receive. Chapter 8 contains more information on rewards and recognition of volunteers. Some libraries provide the following:

- Discounts on book purchases after a period of service.
- No overdue fines on library materials with a complimentary library card.
- Invitations to special events and appreciation parties.
- Job references.
- The opportunity to attend training classes with staff.
- Tax deductions for unreimbursed expenditures given in service to a qualifying organization. Examples of deductible expenses include automobile mileage, bus fares, parking, etc. A

complete description of federal deductions for volunteers can be obtained from the IRS office.
- Discounted bus passes, reserved parking, or other transportation options especially for volunteers or staff.
- Study credit for students or fulfillment of service requirements for civic organizations.

INTRODUCTION TO TRAINING

Effective training, whether for staff or volunteers, has certain qualities. In order to learn, people must gather or be exposed to information, and they must process it. Most people prefer to have a logical sequence to their training and to be told what will happen. Additionally, if they have an opportunity to express their current knowledge and their concerns, they set the scene for additional learning.

Demonstrations, explanations, true stories, and examples enable students full play with the content of their training. Drills in class in addition to subsequent practices permit training to become assimilated. Good training allows control and self-direction in the learning process, shows relationships between experience and new skills, and gives participants an opportunity to participate actively in a practical situation. To encourage the best in all participants, training sessions are informal, friendly, and nonthreatening. To make learning easier, information is repeated and feedback is given in frequent but different formats. Students are encouraged to ask questions, make comments, and share perspectives.

Unfortunately time is limited for staff and volunteers. Several shorter sessions will have a greater impact on learning than one long session. So training is best scheduled in one- or two-hour segments and repeated regularly. This also enables you to tailor sessions to the needs of a particular group of participants, to use training as a tool for reward and recognition, and build increasing levels of expertise. Consider an annual calendar of classes—orientation, forms and record keeping, staff-volunteer relationships, volunteers with special needs, training volunteers, and similar topics.

The goal of training is to imbue students with qualities that enable them to perform at their best. These include coping with change, taking responsibility, working together, developing as individuals and as a unit, and maximizing critical thinking.

SPECIALIZED TRAINING FOR STAFF DEALING WITH VOLUNTEERS WHO HAVE SPECIAL NEEDS

VOLUNTEERS WITH DISABILITIES

Federal and state legislation now require a greater degree of accessibility and service than ever before. They serve to underscore what libraries always have believed—that all who can benefit from libraries should be able to use them. Volunteerism is no exception.

Many agencies, including libraries, have official policies in regard to facilities, equipment, and services for persons with disabilities. This is an excellent starting point for your work with volunteers. You may want to gather more information about local resources. Begin with agencies like social services departments, federal offices with jurisdiction in your city, referral or self-help associations.

Persons with disabilities constitute a pool of potential volunteers that most of us haven't tapped heavily. Your recruitment techniques should be targeted to reach this group. Equally important, however, is advance preparation of staff to work with these individuals. Many of us are initially uncomfortable around people who are different than we are. The following lists some suggestions in dealing with people with disabilities.

1. Meet personally with the staff supervisor to discuss the volunteers you may be placing. Talk about their strengths, skills, and physical requirements. Determine what volunteer tasks can be assigned and if any modifications are needed in the work station or process.

2. Through the supervisor, arrange a gathering with the general staff. This can be formal or informal and conducted by the supervisor or you, depending upon need. Staff should have the opportunity to ask questions and express concerns as well as learn of the particular requirements of a given volunteer.

3. Ensure that all staff are familiar with guidelines for volunteers with physical disabilities. These can be conveyed in new staff orientations, regular training, or briefing sessions for current employees, and in print.

4. Check back to see how the placement is going. Talk to the volunteer and the staff. Keep your door and your phone line open

to more confidential comments and incorporate appropriate suggestions into your program.

GUIDELINES FOR WORKING WITH VOLUNTEERS WHO ARE DISABLED

The following lists describe how to interact and accommodate volunteers who are developmentally disabled and visually, hearing, and mobility impaired.

Volunteers Who Have Mobility Impairments

- Ask before you give assistance.
- Unless a power wheelchair breaks down, you needn't offer to push it. (Power chairs are heavy and hard to steer by hand.) The wheelchair user can maneuver the chair on his or her own.
- If the person who is disabled is accompanied, don't talk only to one or the other person. Speak to both people equally.
- Know the location of the nearest wheelchair-accessible bathroom.
- Check the bathroom if an inordinate amount of break time has passed. The volunteer may need assistance in maneuvering in tight spaces.
- Never pat a person in a wheelchair on the head. The volunteer is neither a pet nor a child.
- Never take a person's crutches or cane away. The volunteer should store the devices under his or her seat, not in the aisle.
- If a volunteer is unsteady on his or her feet, offer your arm. Remember that stairs without hand rails and ramps can be difficult to manage.
- Don't refer to the companion of a person with a disability as an "attendant" or "assistant."

Volunteers Who Are Visually Impaired

- Guide dogs may accompany their owners and sit at their feet.
- Do not pet a guide dog while it is working.
- The correct way to provide sighted guide service to a person who is blind is to offer him or her the opportunity to hold your elbow. This way, you walk slightly in front of the person you are guiding.
- When giving directions to a person who is visually impaired, estimate the distance in steps and use clear, specific language— for example, "To get to the women's bathroom, you need to turn left and follow this curving wall until it ends"; or, "Continue to walk straight for about twenty steps.")

- When guiding the individual, keep conversation to a minimum. He or she imprints directions while travels to remember the route.

Volunteers Who Are Hearing Impaired

Few hearing-impaired people identify themselves, so it is a good idea to use these techniques with all volunteers:

- Face the volunteer when you are speaking to him.
- Position yourself so your face is in good light.
- Keep your hand away from your face when you are speaking. Speak clearly—don't mumble.

Volunteers Who Are Developmentally Disabled

- If a person with a developmental disability has never been to the library, she may not know the expected behavior. State your expectations clearly using short sentences.
- If a person's behavior is disruptive to others, handle the situation at once. Quickly, quietly, and firmly instruct the person in correct behavior.
- Speak to a volunteer with a developmental disability as you would any other volunteer, only use simpler sentences and words.

STAFF SUPERVISORS TRAINING

Prior to providing training for staff supervisors, the right people must be selected. Naturally, staff should have some voice in the decision to name supervisors. In other words, they should be volunteers who have a commitment to volunteerism. From this initial indication of interest, you can evaluate the person based on personality and approach.

Most good supervisors like people and enjoy helping others learn. Supervisors feel they receive as much back as they give when working with volunteers. They are good at communicating as well as being good at their library jobs, and about knowing the agency as a whole. They aren't afraid to ask for help or advice, to admit they are wrong, or to offer praise. They see the big picture; at the same time they don't lose sight of details and procedures.

Qualities that produce any good manager are identical to the ones that constitute a good supervisor of volunteers—only more so.

He should be friendly, supportive, flexible, responsible, and well-organized. In addition, she should possess a fortuitous combination of leadership, authority, and organizational skills. Regardless of the actual job classification of a supervisor, personality traits determine the success of her charge. Supervisors need support and guidance as much as they require training. But if you provide initial and periodic classes, you will build their confidence at the same time you fine-tune their skills.

The volunteer director has the ability to confirm or veto staff supervisors, and offer training to individuals and through group or workshop sessions. Training should incorporate the points in the general section on training previously mentioned but specifically targeted to staff supervisors. Frequently it must be individualized to a specific setting or type of activity. What should be included in supervisors' training? Start by deciding what supervisors should do at your library.

Take the tasks your library assigns to supervisors and incorporate those points in your training. Some are appropriate for advanced training, too.

- Serve as the initial and ongoing contact for volunteers.
- Define work and apply acceptable standards.
- Make actual assignments.
- Keep records and send them to the Volunteer Office.
- Conduct orientations and training at a department or branch.
- Plan reward and recognition efforts.
- Handle evaluations/appraisals, problems and conflicts.

TIPS FOR SUPERVISORY OPERATIONS

Supervisors manage regular types of activities and should be comfortable conducting them. Particular areas of operations include orientation, initial assignments, conferences, evaluations, record keeping, dealing with conflicts and disagreements, and personal development.

Orientation

Many of the points listed in the section on orientation (above) are conducted by the immediate supervisor. The volunteer director and the supervisor should agree which details each will cover. In addition to familiarizing the volunteer with the library and its functions, the supervisor is establishing a relationship with the volunteer and learning about his interests and skills.

Initial Assignment

If the volunteer has not already received specific duties, the supervisor works with her to make that assignment. It's helpful if the supervisor keeps an ongoing list of tasks and projects that volunteers can do and relays these occasionally to the volunteer director. The supervisor should clearly define the job's duties, expectations, and rules. He or she also helps the volunteer decide on a schedule, goals, and related items.

Conferences and Evaluations

To discuss changes, plans, and projects that affect the entire agency, volunteers can be included in staff meetings. Training and delegation of tasks may be handled either in a group or individually. Appraisals and evaluations should be conducted in private sessions where candidness is encouraged. Conferences or evaluations should be scheduled regularly, and additional times as needed. In particular, try to correct mistakes immediately in a constructive manner and be willing to demonstrate several methods for doing a job.

Record-Keeping

The supervisor should maintain current, accurate records in compliance with the Volunteer Office's requirements. It's easiest to accomplish this by making the volunteers responsible for entering their own time, hours, activities, and other information, when possible. However, the supervisor should make spot checks to make certain that information is accurate. Some supervisors add additional points to track trends or obtain extra details. Remember that record-keeping includes maintaining personal registers with emergency contacts. The supervisor's statistics concerning community service workers are an additional safeguard for this group of volunteers. Figure 5-2 is an example of a Volunteer Contribution Record.

Conflicts and Disagreements

The supervisor should be prepared to handle conflicts that arise, either on his or her own or through involvement of a third party. These may range from minor matters such as schedules to major tension resulting from ongoing personality conflicts. [See chapter 10, Problem-Solving Assessment]

Personal Development

Volunteers, like employees, become bored and unmotivated when not challenged. Some people need occasional change in their assignments, some want opportunities to learn new skills, and others

---

FIGURE 5-2: Volunteer Contribution Record

Volunteer Contribution Record

Name _____ Library Dept. _____

Address _____ Night Phone _____

City _____ State _____ Zip _____ Day Phone _____

Position _____

This form may be used to list in-kind contributions and expenses incurred while serving as a volunteer. Do not include expenses for which you are reimbursed.

Date   Description   Amount

_____

_____

_____

_____

_____

                                              TOTAL _____

Complete the form, attach receipts, sign and date it, and give to your volunteer supervisor. The supervisor will document the items and send a copy to the Volunteer Office and to you.

This form presents an accurate record of my contributions.

Volunteer _____ Date _____

I verify that these contributions were provided for services to the Library.

Supervisor _____ Date _____

Reviewed by Volunteer Director _____ Date _____

are eager for additional responsibility. The supervisor is mentor and guide in this process and needs to discern when a volunteer is ready for new duties and challenges.

TRAINING VOLUNTEERS

Specific training for volunteers is provided by the volunteer director, a staff supervisor, project directors, or another volunteer—whoever is best capable of teaching as well as knowledgeable about the tasks. Training should be flexible to meet the schedules of the trainer and the volunteer as well as to capitalize on the volunteer's strengths, interests, and experience.

To guide your training, consider the following steps. This process can be applied to any level or type of training.

1. Be familiar with job descriptions; expand in detail on the tasks you need completed and list them in writing, along with essential information and skills.

2. Develop training objectives that are observable and measurable; also acceptable conditions for completion of tasks.

3. Decide the content of training, drawing upon the expertise of other people to assist you. What needs to come first? Which parts build upon preceding proficiency?

4. Establish the methods for training. Consider options like training manuals, audio/video support, lectures, hands-on, role playing, and others.

5. Calculate the amount of time for each training method along with the schedule you will need to meet conditions.

6. Decide how you will evaluate the success of the training program. Ability to perform the job? Numbers of volunteers? Follow-up with participants?

7. List the equipment, materials and people you require to produce the training and procure them.

8. Implement training, evaluate it, and revise. Training is an on-going process.

Consider an example of the training process from the Denver Public Library. The Denver Public Library is converting the method of tracking its collection to a bar-coding system. This involves entering the item's assigned number on computer, which produces a numbered self-stick label for the worker to place on the corner of the material. The worker frequently also reshelves the item in order.

To produce training, the volunteer director first created a written job description based on discussions with the project supervisor. Together, they determined that no particular educational background or skills would be required, although some familiarity with computers was desirable and ability to understand the Dewey Decimal System was important.

Training objectives included a sufficient amount of time to learn the tasks with resulting accuracy and satisfactory number of items converted. Content of training was based on training provided personally to the volunteer director by the supervisor and other staff. Because the tasks involved are routine and sequential, it was decided that a hands-on approach to training was best for all of the volunteers. The amount of time for the training was determined through actual trial and experience as staff and volunteers began the project. A variable based on schedules and volunteers' needs was the number trained at a given session, ranging from one to four or five.

An evaluation of the success of the training was based on numbers of items that are being converted accurately. Equipment is permanently installed on site, materials are provided by staff, and trainers include the volunteer director and the staff supervisor, depending upon schedules. Training is continuous and can be revised to fit the situation until all items are bar-coded.

This example shows that training need not be difficult to plan and implement. You probably already observe the sequence of steps for most of your training methods. The checklist above shows if you are including each essential point.

JOINT TRAINING ON VOLUNTEER-STAFF RELATIONS

The training that should receive priority your volunteer program is volunteer/staff relations. By providing training to encourage teamwork, you can address this consideration before minor irritations grow to major problems. A workshop for staff and volunteers encourages candor, identifies issues, and monitors the degree of acceptance of volunteers by staff. The Denver Public Library has developed a structure for a ninety-minute workshop that can serve as a guide for your own session. The format can be adapted to other training topics, too.

Schedule the workshop at the optimum time for high attendance. Promote participation through newsletter articles, flyers, and support from management. New employees should be required to attend. Other preliminaries are to set up the room for maximum interaction (circles are good); provide light refreshments; double-check all supplies and equipment; greet arrivals personally; provide name tags; use a flip chart as a group memory for goals, issues, and suggestions.

1. Introductions (15 minutes)
- Visit with a fellow participant
- Leader lists goals of workshop on chart
- Share a concern about volunteer/staff relationships

Participants introduce themselves to the group, where they work, what they do, what they hope to gain from the workshop. The leader explains why the training is being held, what will occur, and how it will benefit participants. An example of a goal: this workshop will help you understand how your job fits within your department and the library.

You may be surprised by the issues that surface in the brainstorming session. Some items that you assumed create friction may turn out to be nonissues. In our workshops, we have discovered interesting items.

Issues To Volunteers:

- A place of their own.
- Access to supplies.
- Being up-to-date on activities and general library matters.
- Variety of things to do.
- Clear definition of tasks.
- Good communication.

Issues To Staff:

- Finding time to train volunteers.
- Getting to know volunteers, especially teenagers.
- Ways to show ongoing appreciation.

- How to provide orientation.
- Legal responsibilities.
- Task assignments that aren't popular.
- Balancing social and task needs.
- Evaluating the work of volunteers.
- "Supplement, not supplant" employees.
- Finding jobs that challenge and motivate.
- Working with diverse personalities.

Issues To Both:

- Choices of tasks.
- Identifying staff and volunteers (name tags).
- Cramped quarters.
- Working as a team when you don't know each other.

2. **Review of volunteerism (5 minutes)**
   - What volunteerism means—past and present.
   - Agency's philosophy.

3. **What do volunteers and staff want? (15 minutes)**
   - Brainstorm individually the qualities sought in work situation.
   - Share results in small groups.
   - Prioritize topics in a large group.
   - Discuss similarities between the groups.

4. **Building volunteer jobs that motivate. (15 minutes)**
   - Assign teams of both volunteers and staff.
   - Design an "ideal" volunteer job.
   - Share highlights in large group.
   - Discuss other ways to provide a motivating atmosphere.

Break. (5 minutes)

5. **Communication at work. (10 minutes)**
   Components of communication—listening, clarifying and interpreting, providing information, supporting by checking back, reinforcing.

6. **Strategies to improve relations. (5 minutes)**
   Brainstorm and list actions that can be taken.

7. **Overview of volunteer positions and tasks. (10 minutes)**

8. **Recruitment. (5 minutes)**
   Enlist participants in recruitment of volunteers by highlighting desired skills and important projects.

9. **Evaluation of workshop. (5 minutes)**
   Check original goals on flip chart.
   Provide written form for each participant (positives, points for improvement, possible future topics).

10. **Presentation of certificates as participants exit.**
    Certificates are a good method to round out the workshop. They give participants a sense of accomplishment and provide a tangible record. Other tips for the workshop:

    - Begin and end on time.
    - Break topics into easily assimilated, short segments of fifteen minutes or less.
    - Use a variety of training methods and encourage individual participation and sharing.
    - Provide handouts and fact sheets for use after the session.
    - Create a resource table with general volunteer and library information.

6 EVALUATIONS AND RECORDS

It has been said that just because a thing can be counted, does not mean that it should be counted. This is a perfect illustration of the method by which we all too often judge success and failure.

Instead of counting quantities, with the volunteer program evaluated by a ten percent increase in people or a 35 percent increase in hours, we advocate evaluations based on two criteria:

1. Does the measurement give us information that we need to adequately guide the volunteer program? (Please note that in this case, not meeting a goal can provide information even more valuable than achieving it.)
2. Does the appraisal focus on quality? Quality delivery of service along with satisfaction of volunteers and staff?

Any evaluation is better than none; so if you're at the number-counting stage, that's fine. You've made a beginning. Keep in mind the variety of additional methods you might use and try one or more different ways to evaluate:

- Volunteers of the volunteer program in general.
- Volunteers of their particular assignment.
- Volunteers of themselves.
- Volunteers of staff.
- Staff of the volunteer program in general.
- Staff of particular volunteer components.
- Staff of volunteers.
- Staff supervisors of themselves.
- Management of cost-effectiveness and additional benefits.
- Customers of service utilizing volunteers.

These are some of the options; you may think of more. Don't fear that you will spend all of your time compiling reports. Don't shrug your shoulders at the bewildering array. By moving one step at a time, and establishing procedures and timelines in advance, many forms of evaluations can become a small part of your regular routine.

HOW DO YOU SPELL "SUCCESS"?

The first step in obtaining evaluations is to have a clear idea of what you're trying to achieve. This probably is contained, or at least implied, in the goals and objectives (stated or unstated) for a specific activity.

EVALUATION ACTIVITY EXAMPLE

This example shows that the volunteer program needs reasonable expectations and a global view in order to determine "success."

A branch library decides to sponsor a local storyteller as a program for children and parents. A staff member calls your office for volunteers to take flyers to five neighboring shops and to welcome, usher, bring cookies, serve refreshments, and clean up. You decide you'll recruit two people to distribute flyers, four to bake cookies, and six to help at the event. Check all results that qualify the event as a success:

1. _____ Ten people show up to distribute flyers to shops.
2. _____ Twenty boys, girls, and parents attend.
3. _____ No one gets food poisoning from the cookies.
4. _____ The neighborhood witch volunteers to usher.
5. _____ Double the number of audience members drop by than can be seated.
6. _____ Out of the three volunteers needed to serve refreshments, only one actually appears.
7. _____ Out of three volunteers needed to serve refreshments, all three appear, but they stand behind the table gossiping.

Answers:
   1. Probably not a success. Although you may need some extra help as a precaution, in this instance too many people will feel they have wasted their time. You should have screened them first or called to suggest another option.
   2. Could be a success, it all depends. Is this the first time for the event? Does attendance show a need to increase the numbers of flyers that volunteers distribute? Did the audience enjoy themselves? The volunteer component needs to be evaluated in context.

3. An unqualified success! All too often we forget the real disasters that might occur except for our care.

4. Maybe, maybe not. Have you converted her to a friend by giving her a new opportunity to shine? Or does she continue scaring small children, thereby driving your customers away?

5. Edging toward the negative. Customer satisfaction and effective delivery of services are the library's ultimate purposes. If half the audience is disgruntled, you're pushing it. But again, the volunteer component should be evaluated in context with other factors.

6. Was one out of three sufficient? More important, did refreshments get served no matter what happened, and was the event as a whole successful? Sometimes we forget the ultimate goal in a fog of details.

7. Failure. Even if you've toted up three work-hours for your annual total, your library has lost ground. In addition to not filling their agreements, the volunteers may have alienated customers or staff by their attitude.

METHODOLOGY

Regardless of the evaluation, its format, subjects, or timing, you are seeking two things:

1. INDIVIDUAL satisfaction and ideas for improvement.
2. TRENDS that can be extrapolated from groups and categories of evaluations. These might be for a particular location, activity, age, or whatever.

Concrete suggestions or comments can be passed along to the appropriate person, whether favorable or unfavorable. Don't forget to honor anonymity if you promise it or if it's requested. A number of responses to a questionnaire can be consolidated into statistical reports, numbers or percentages that rank the volunteer program as "good," for example. These can be further segmented according to demographics, life style, or geographic area — for example, opinions of seniors as compared to young mothers, or people working at a certain branch, or those holding memberships in other cultural organizations. Ultimately what we are talking about is a solid computer program to analyze data along with really good entry skills by someone in your office.

Maybe you lack a great computer program or the staff to enter data. That's all right; do the best you can with what you have.

You probably have gut feelings for some of these items. See if you can validate them through evaluations.

EVALUATIONS OF PEOPLE

Evaluations usually contain referrals to programs, goals, and people. They are a combination of questions and points of view. People ask some basic questions of themselves and others when evaluating the human resource, as it's now known. What are expectations of individuals? Why is fulfilling that function important? Do people have the authority or an impact on the activity? Who else is involved or can help? And finally, what is the individual's effectiveness in accomplishing goals?

Basing a person's evaluation on only the last question is unfair and misleading. That is why evaluations must be part of the management continuum forward and backward. Evaluations must be weighed along with other factors when you are deciding on the structure or process of the volunteer program.

EVALUATIONS BY VOLUNTEERS

Evaluations by volunteers are the same as feedback interviews. The evaluations should be conducted after a short interval following the volunteer's initial placement and regularly thereafter. Although an interview conducted in person or by telephone by the director of volunteers or a representative is preferable because of the nuances you can obtain and the depths you can probe, you can mail the printed form if necessary.

The purpose of this evaluation is primarily to guarantee that the match between the volunteer and project fits, rather than obtain assessments of the volunteer program overall or specific volunteer activities. It helps you deal with concerns up front.

The questions you should include cover the volunteer's relationship to a supervisor, to other staff and volunteers; amount of work; proper scheduling; adequate training; strengths or benefits of the job; things that could be improved; other concerns; overall job satisfaction. Figure 6-1 is an example of a "One Month Evaluation Form."

From these questions you can determine when the volunteer needs additional guidance or assistance. A copy of the evaluation is sent to the supervisor when the evaluation is complete. If problems appear, you should discuss these in detail with the supervisor. One young lady at a Denver library, full of enthusiasm for her assignment, took responsibility for mailings. Over the first few weeks she performed well. However as time went on she gradu-

---

FIGURE 6-1: Volunteer's One Month Evaluation Form

Name _____ Work Location _____

Assignment _____ Supervisor _____

Beginning Date _____ Date of Orientation _____

Daytime Phone _____ Best time to call _____

☐ Relationship to Supervisor:

☐ Relationship to team members:

☐ Response to work load (too much or too little):

☐ Response to hours:

☐ Quality of On-the-job training:

☐ Job strengths:

☐ Job weaknesses:

☐ Concerns:

☐ Overall job satisfaction:

NEED FOR FOLLOW UP? NO _____ YES _____ (if so, when?) _____

Phone Interviewer _____ Date _____

ally became discouraged and her donated time diminished considerably. Questioned at her one month evaluation, she said she consistently ran out of envelopes, and neither she nor the staff on duty had access to supplies. This quick evaluation revealed two easily solved problems: (1) the volunteer worked faster than anticipated, and additional responsibilities could be assigned; (2) easier access to supplies needed to be arranged.

ONE YEAR AND PERIODIC FOLLOWING EVALUATIONS

At the end of their first year, and periodically thereafter, volunteers are asked to complete an evaluation of the Volunteer Program. Volunteers receive the evaluation through the mail so that they can document their feelings anonymously if they want. Although portions can cover personal relationships, by and large this effort is directed toward tracking the links between progress from the individual to institution. Figure 6-2 is an example of an evaluation of the volunteer program form.

Periodic evaluations are important because people and situations change over time. A retired secretary originally requested clerical duties. She was given newspaper clippings to file. At her one-year evaluation, she revealed that her greatest enjoyment came from *reading* the items she filed. Subsequently she took charge of preparing an index of clippings as well as filing them.

Unfortunately, almost any volunteer will quietly disappear if something is out of tune at a placement—She won't complain and he won't confront. You must take the initiative and use evaluations, interviews, and assessments to help you pinpoint staff members or volunteers that may need additional training, or transfer responsibilities for staff supervision to someone more interested, or determine when a volunteer needs new challenges. The following example describes how one situation was handled.

A retired woman had been the mainstay of a library department for five years, coming in three times a week like clockwork. Death, promotions, and transfers changed the staff composition in her office, and she began working with a new clerk whose procedures and priorities were different. Her inclination was to disappear one morning and never return. An intervention was conducted by a supervisor and that cleared the air and clarified expectations for both parties.

FIGURE 6-2: Volunteer Program Evaluation Form

EVALUATION OF THE VOLUNTEER PROGRAM BY VOLUNTEER

Volunteer's Name (optional): _____

Job Description: _____ Department _____

(PRIVATE)	Poor	Fair	Good	Excellent
To what extent did the description of your job represent what needed to be done?				
To what extent do you feel your job utilizes your talents and satisfies your reason for becoming a DPL volunteer?				
To what extent do you feel you are receiving support from your supervisor?				
Rate your relationships with team members:				
To what extent do you feel that the paid staff in this organization have acknowledged and appreciated your volunteer contribution?				

Thing I have particularly enjoyed about being a DPL volunteer:

Things I wish had been different:

Additional comments:

Date:

EXIT INTERVIEWS

Whenever possible, an exit interview is given when the volunteer completes the volunteer term. These can be the most instructive evaluations you receive, so do your best to obtain them and stress to volunteers the importance of completing them. You should ask for positives as well as negatives, suggestions for changes, an overview of accomplishments, and suggestions for desirable skills. A copy of these documents should be sent to the supervisor. Figure 6-3 is an example of a Volunteer Exit Overview form.

EVALUATING SPECIAL PROJECTS OR EVENTS

The most difficult evaluation to obtain concerns special projects or events. It frequently is almost impossible to get formal feedback, either verbal or written, from volunteers who flee like the wind after a project is completed. One option is to make comment cards available throughout the term of the project—stacked on the table at a street fair or handed to each volunteer when he or she leaves. A clipboard with writing paper accomplishes the same thing if you head it with "Comments, Ideas, Concerns."

This should be paired with regular post-activity evaluations by staff. If you normally participate in such sessions, an overview of what went right and wrong with the volunteer component can easily be included. Otherwise, conduct your own review, even with a few phone calls, and *summarize the findings in writing* for the next project.

Gossip? Idle conversation? These carry validity, too, and can be captured by alert listeners. On a research project headed by two volunteers, these highly capable women listened to the comments of other volunteers who were identifying subjects in photos. They expanded the scope of the project to include additional information useful to researchers in years to come.

EVALUATIONS BY STAFF

Employees transform objectives into projects and activities, words into actions. Gaining staff opinions is essential not only to make them feel like part of the process (read "buy-in") but also because the volunteer staff has immediate, front-line experience in what is going right or wrong.

Evaulations of individuals usually are designed to track satisfaction of the volunteer and staff with the assignment. When the initial evaluation of the volunteer is performed by the Volunteer Director, the immediate supervisor should be encouraged also to

Figure 6-3: Volunteer Exit Overview

VOLUNTEER EXIT OVERVIEW

Name _____

Address _____

City/Zip _____

Length of service: Beginning _____ Ending _____

Reason for leaving _____

_____

_____

1. What are the positive aspects of volunteering at the Denver Public Library?
2. What are the negative aspects of volunteering at the Denver Public Library?
3. What accomplishments are you most proud of?
4. What professional skills were you able to utilize or gain?
5. What frustrated you most while volunteering?

    a. Suggest the way(s) in which the frustration could have been alleviated.

    b. Suggestions for improving/changing the program:

6. Would you be willing to volunteer with the Denver Public Library in the future? Why or why not?
7. Would you recommend the program?   YES _____ NO _____

(CONFIDENTIAL) RATE THE FOLLOWING:	Poor	Fair	Good	Excellent
Your experience as a volunteer				
Quality of supervision				
Relationships with others in unit				
Quality of On-the-Job training				
Support from the Volunteer Office (Newsletter, calls, cards/letters, etc.)				
Recognition from the unit				

Additional comments:

conduct an informal assessment, similar to an employee evaluation so he or she can chart progress or handle any difficulties before they get too large. Other staff can get involved, too. After a sensitive project in which a person with disabilities worked closely with a small group of employees, a librarian drafted an entire set of suggestions for improving staff-volunteer relationships for this special situation. Many of these suggestion are covered further in Chapter 5 on Orientation and Training.

HOW OFTEN

At a minimum, evaluations of volunteers should be conducted annually. When an evaluation interview is due, a form is sent to the supervisor. Figure 6-4 is an example of an annual evaluation of volunteer form. Supervisors are asked, whenever possible, to complete the interview with the volunteer and return it to the Volunteer Office by the end of the month in which they receive it. The evaluation interview allows the volunteer and the supervisor the opportunity to share feelings about the success of the placement and to do planning. The interview helps to ensure that the expectations of the library and volunteer are being met.

Regular evaluations of volunteers should continue thereafter because people change and situations lose their appeal. Unless you provide an opportunity for feedback, your program may fall victim to the "gradual erosion" syndrome.

Evaluation interviews should also be conducted any time there is a performance problem as a problem-solving and documentation tool. The problem-solving assessment form (see Figure 10-1, Chapter 10) can help pinpoint problems and alternative solutions.

STAFF APPRAISAL OF THE PROGRAM OVERALL

The final area you will find useful to review is the opinion of staff about the volunteer program overall. Brace yourself—this means *you* will be evaluated, too.

Naturally you'll want to adapt the following suggestions to your own situation. But consider querying staff about areas like the following:

Volunteers: Are they sufficiently trained? Usually well-matched to tasks? Reliable? Are volunteers well utilized? How could this be done better? What benefits do they bring? What problems do they create?

FIGURE 6-4: Annual Evaluation of Volunteer

ANNUAL EVALUATION OF VOLUNTEER

Job Description: _____ Department _____

Period of Feedback: _____

(CONFIDENTIAL) Checklist of Volunteer Work Characteristics	Poor	Fair	Good	Excellent
To what extent does the volunteer demonstrate the knowledge essential to the present job classification?				
To what extent does the volunteer organize work so that it is done accurately and efficiently?				
To what extent does the volunteer apply his or her resources in·order to accomplish what is assigned?				
How successful is the volunteer in altering activities to meet the demands of new situations?				
To what extent can the volunteer be depended upon to be punctual, present at work, and/or follows through with contacting supervisor when absent?				
How successful is he or she in getting along with people in daily work relationships?				

A. Describe area(s) of strong performance:

B. Describe area(s) which could be improved:

C. How does performance during this rating period compare with prior rating?

FIGURE 6-4: Continued

Overall comments by interviewer:

Comments by Volunteer:

_____

Supervisor:

_____
Please PRINT name

_____
Signature   Date

 Volunteer:

_____
Please PRINT name

_____
Signature   Date

Staff: What role do they play with volunteers? Do they have access to sufficient training? Do they work well with volunteers? Has the work load increased or decreased (or changed) because of the presence of volunteers?

Volunteer Office: Is enough assistance given with volunteers? Are there tasks or projects for volunteers that should be added or dropped?

A survey of this type might be conducted every year or two. It also could be most effective when rotated with discussion or focus groups with opportunities for more intensive interaction and comments. Some suggestions made by staff via surveys that were implemented at the Denver Public Library are as follows:

- regular inquiries to ask about their volunteer needs;
- more training for staff, and;
- more specialized training for certain volunteers.

Surveys also verified that many activities directed by the Volunteer Office were already outstanding.

Figure 6-5 is an example of a staff assessment of the volunteer program form.

EVALUATIONS OF STAFF

Now that we've considered evaluations by volunteers, evaluations of volunteers, and evaluations of programs or projects, we need to consider staff evaluations. You may want to incorporate some questions within the regular forms used by volunteers. Or you may prefer to periodically develop a special survey or form that includes questions on peer employees as well as staff supervisors.

Another system includes work with volunteers as an item upon which staff appraisals are based. This can be accomplished in one of two of the following ways:

1. Include work with volunteers as an expected duty for all, or selected, job descriptions. Accomplishments can then be rated as they would be for any given duty, such as customer service.
2. Use work with volunteers as a supplement to employment evaluations. In this instance, supervising volunteers is additional to regular duties and indicates work above and beyond. It helps the employee qualify for raises and promotions.

Staff can be evaluated on their relationships with volunteers, record-keeping, project or program development, training abilities, and other items. Changes could and should be made based upon evaluations. You may find, as we did, that a staff supervisor worked well with adult volunteers but not with teenagers. Subsequently these youngsters were assigned to work under another staff member.

FIGURE 6-5: Staff Assessment of the Volunteer Program Courtesy of Catherine Childs, Volunteer Office, Boulder Public Library

STAFF ASSESSMENT OF THE VOLUNTEER PROGRAM

Department: _____

As part of our continued effort to improve our volunteer program, we would like your responses to the following questions. Please answer all questions (1 - 13). Do not sign the survey unless you wish to. All responses will be kept confidential.

1. In which capacity are you usually involved with volunteers in your area?
   ____ work with them directly   ____ observation only
   ____ no involvement   ____ supervise staff who work with volunteers

2. In your experience, are the volunteers referred to your area appropriate for their assignments?
   ____ yes   ____ usually   ____ not usually   ____ no   ____ don't know

3. How would you rate the utilization of volunteers in your area?
   ____ generally well utilized   ____ generally not well utilized
   ____ don't know
   How could they be better utilized? _____
   _____
   _____

4. Are the volunteers in your department adequately prepared or trained for their responsibilities?
   ____ most are   ____ some are/some aren't   ____ most aren't

5. Do you think the staff members in your area generally work well with volunteers?
   ____ yes   ____ no

6. How would you describe the reaction of our patrons to the volunteers?
   ____ generally favorable   ____ mixed   ____ generally not favorable
   ____ don't know
   Any specific comments or suggestions? _____

7. What benefits do you think we have gained by using volunteers?
   _____
   _____
   _____

8. What problems have we created by using volunteers?
   _____
   _____
   _____

9. How has your own work load increased or decreased as a result of utilizing volunteers?
   ____ decreased   ____ increased   ____ remained the same

   Has the nature of your duties changed for the better?
   ____ yes   ____ no   ____ remained the same

FIGURE 6-5: Continued

10. How would you describe the assistance you have received from the volunteer services coordinator?
    ____ generally helpful   ____ somewhat helpful   ____ generally not helpful

11. Please describe any general volunteer roles or specific volunteer tasks that you would like to see added to the opportunities available to volunteers now:
    _____
    _____

12. Are there any current volunteer opportunities which you would like to see discontinued?
    ____ yes   ____ no
    If so, why? _____
    _____
    _____

13. Please describe any suggestions you have for the (Volunteer Office) to make it easier and more rewarding for you to meet your volunteer needs or work with volunteers on a day to day basis: _____
    _____
    _____
    _____
    _____

    ADDITIONAL COMMENTS: _____
    _____
    _____

Name (optional): _____
(If you would like to have a follow-up discussion with the Volunteer Office)

ANALYZING MATERIALS AND METHODS

People are not the only items that can be evaluated. In many ways, tangible items and particular activities are easier to analyze because initial results can be counted. How many people responded to a notice in a newspaper? Did you recruit suitable potential volunteers by appearing at a community fair?

Any time you or support staff can track responses, you should do so. A potential volunteer who contacts you should be asked where he heard about your program. Participants at a community fair should jot a note about each recruit they've talked to—including obvious demographic information. When you mass mail brochures, try to code them according to market segments—for example, a mailing list may consist of young mothers at home, working parents, or single parents—use a colored marker to note which group this was mailed to on the return form, and count the numbers of responses from particular zip codes or neighborhoods.

However, be careful not to jump to conclusions based on results. A low response to a particular newspaper notice may be based on the time of year it ran or the types of activities it listed. A high response to a mailing may be from an attractive design rather than a strong interest in a particular program. Items like printed or audio-visual materials can be analyzed not only by response to them but also may benefit from a review by disinterested people or experts in advertising and publications.

RECORD-KEEPING

Each method of evaluation ultimately can have an impact on your volunteer effort. Whether you are counting or surveying, you are obtaining valuable information. But how do you put it all together?

You will need to keep separate files on each regular volunteer with original skills forms or applications, letters of commendation, evaluations, and copies of other forms. But ultimately the most efficient way to track and compile information is via computer.

Computer Evaluation Programs

What should a really good computer program do? It should replace the long, tedious hours you've spent using pencil, paper, and a calculator and it should be easy to learn. You should be able to call up lists of people based upon interests, skills, age, residence, employment, days and times of availability, and other criteria. These are called "fields."

After you've entered hours and activities, the computer should be able to spit back various reports: daily, weekly, monthly, yearly by numbers of hours, numbers of volunteers, activity, skill, and so forth. It should provide mailing labels categorized by alphabet, zip, or field. Ideally, you can also match individuals with pieces of correspondence, so you can send thank-you notes or birthday cards addressed personally.

Commercial programs are available, or a computer whiz may be able to adapt an existing program. Make sure that your computer programmer talks at length with the director of volunteers before formatting the record files.

Programmers sometimes seem to speak a foreign language. Because you may not be familiar with computer equipment and terminology, it can be difficult to agree on computer services for the Volunteer Office. Try turning the process around. Start with the completed information you think you may need to track in the next years: ages; demographics; hours per month; and what kind of information will you want to be able to report, access, or summarize? The programmer should work with this, broken down into as many small separate pieces as possible.

BEYOND MERE NUMBERS

How many volunteers do you have and how many hours did they donate this year? Answers in numbers are one way to begin record-keeping. But a tally of hours served without an analysis of accomplishments is not worth its computer time. Where should you begin?

By stating measurable objectives for the entire volunteer program itself, you can assess if goals were met. A yearly evaluation of the program is best, and we suggest that these areas be measured.

1. The actual quantity and quality of the work done by volunteers, if possible by job description or type of work—for example: Activity—book repair, two hours per week, repaired one hundred books.
2. The accomplishments of the volunteer management team, not just numbers of volunteers used, but incorporating management matters such as the demographic composition of the volunteer corps, types and results of recruitment outreach efforts, and so forth.
3. The type and degree of service provided to staff by volunteers and the Volunteer Office. This probably includes a monetary figure.
4. The benefits to the whole organization from volunteer involvement.

The answers to these points can be explicated as well as quantified. For example, you can determine if objectives have been met or exceeded in a matter of degrees from poor to excellent. Quantities explained by details—task types and clarification—give you a better picture of results.

This process is also applicable to specific projects, activities, or tasks. You may want a snapshot of the performance of volunteers who are working as staff aides. By adapting an evaluation form, obtaining opinions of volunteers and staff, and compiling results into an inclusive answer, you get a comprehensive perspective of the situation. You may find that two-thirds of volunteer staff aides are satisfied with their training, but only one-third of paid staff are — a discrepancy that should be investigated.

DIRECTIONS FROM EVALUATIONS

As your record-keeping becomes more sophisticated, you can plug in indicators that are based on information gathered. It takes a period of time to track these propensities, but the data will alert you to potential trouble spots. Consider items such as the rate of turnover in specific assignments, accomplishments of short-term versus long-term volunteers, and assignments that have been vacant for an unusually long time.

From these points you can begin to develop solutions. For example, if turnover seems to occur monthly in a particular area, perhaps there is a problem with the supervisory staff or the physical environment. At least once a year, you should compare current records to previous ones. Begin to chart changes from year to year to build an agency profile. Figure 6-6 is an example of reporting forms and computer information.

Implementing Evaluation Results

Obviously evaluations are only useful if you use them to improve your program. Improvements can be directly related to a specific service. At the Denver Public Library, a genealogy volunteer noticed that a large list of marriages was indexed by only the husband's name. At his suggestion, volunteers indexed by the wife's name, too. This thousand-hour project provided worthwhile work for many new volunteers and an improvement in service for customers.

Improvements may also be broader. If you find, for example, that you have very few Hispanic volunteers, you can develop a pilot project to test the waters. Try to increase this component using recruitment, promotion, personal contacts, and reinforcements. However, seniors might be your strength. You may decide to go with your strength and use suggestions from evaluations, such as building opportunities for mature individuals, creating car pool support, or starting a "Senior Spotlight" in the newsletter.

It's a good idea to include the people who will be impacted before you make major changes. A short-term committee composed of staff and volunteers can brainstorm exciting new ideas and give you valuable perspective.

FIGURE 6-6: Reporting Forms and Computer Information

Sheet1

MONTH	Regular Total	Docent Total	Community Service Total	Homebound Total	Children	Central	Branch	Special Event	Library Store
JANUARY									
FEBRUARY									
*MARCH									
APRIL									
MAY									
*JUNE									
JULY									
AUGUST									
*SEPTEMBER									
OCTOBER									
NOVEMBER									
*DECEMBER									
TOTAL HOURS									

FIGURE 6-6: Continued

```
                          Print Key Output                          Page
     5738SS1 V2R3M0 931217              DFL

     Display Device  . . . . . :
     User  . . . . . . . . . :

     VMF001-01                DENVER PUBLIC LIBRARY              PROMPT
                      System Reference File Maintenance

        1  Assignment Type          19  Milestone Date Descriptions
        2  Award Status             20  Milestone Status
        3  Award Type               21  Military Branch
        4  Biographical Type        22  Military Rank
        5  Comment Security Levels  23  Military Status
        6  Defaults for Labels      24  Miscellaneous Parameters
        7  Easy Bio Individuals     25  Orientation Status
        8  Easy Bio Organization    26  Owner Of Volunteer
        9  Fiscal Year Parameters   27  Participation Level
       10  Form Of Recognition      28  Phone Type
       11  Geographic Areas         29  Placement Services
       12  Inactivity Status        30  Project Status
       13  Interest/Experience Skills 31 Project Tracking Amount Code
       14  Internal Assignment      32  Project Tracking Count Code
       15  Interview Status         33  Recruitment Type
       16  Label Request Codes      34  Resources
       17  License Status           35  Service Center
       18  License Type             36  Special Needs

     F3=Exit                        Group Number to Maintain
```

```
                          Print Key Output
     5738SS1 V2R3M0 931217              DFL

     Display Device  . . . . . :
     User  . . . . . . . . . :

                              DENVER PUBLIC LIBRARY
     3/09/95                  Volunteer Main Menu
     11:30:30                    Menu: VOL                      Lvl: 1

              1  Volunteer Reference Maintenance
              2  Volunteer Maintenance
              3  Timesheet Maintenance
              4  Volunteer Timesheet Maintenance
              5  SSS Volunteer Maintenance
              6  FREEDOM Reference Maintenance
              7  Biographical Maintenance
              8  Donor Maintenance
              9  Segmentation for Reports and Letters
             11  Volunteer Inquiry Menu
             12  Volunteer Reporting Menu
             13  Volunteer Miscellaneous Processing
             14  Volunteer Projects

         Enter Selection:
                                        Default Output Queue: PRT01
     F5=Main Menu         F8=Work Submitted Jobs    F9=Work spool files
     F10=Display Messages    F12=Previous
                 (C) COPYRIGHT 1991 INFO SYSTEMS OF N.C., INC.
```

THE FINAL EVALUATION

The final evaluation rests on the significance of the entire volunteer effort. Ask yourself some of the following questions. Note the similarity to the questions first posed when the volunteer program was initiated:

- What were we able to accomplish this year because of the extra help from volunteers?
- What did volunteers free staff to do?
- Did we innovate or experiment this year because volunteers agreed to test something new?
- Which assignments are popular with volunteers and why?
- Has our public relations or image changed, and can we trace any of this change to the impact of volunteers?
- Have members of the salaried staff visibly developed their supervisory skills as a result of working with volunteers?
- What branches or offices don't use volunteers? Why not?
- What suggestions or observations are being made by volunteers that might be useful to the library?
- Finally, ask branches and departments to report on volunteer accomplishments.

These kinds of questions give excellent information about overall needs, strategies, and service deserving recognition. It will point out areas of strength as well as weakness.

THE BOTTOM LINE

People in service organizations hate to pin a dollar value on their efforts. We in libraries especially feel that the value of access to information is incalculable. But until the time that virtue is truly its own reward, we must make one measurement: that of monetary value. For people in the field of volunteerism, that task becomes a delight as we tally up the savings to our library from our efforts and the participation of volunteers. We can select from several methods to estimate the value.

Customarily (and easiest) is the minimum wage. Take the number of hours donated by volunteers, multiply by the minimum wage, and *presto,* a value. Although this system is easy, it gives an erroneous view of the value of volunteer services. The second method, established by the National Center of Volunteer Action (Washington, D.C.), assigns a value of $11.48 per hour to be multiplied times numbers of hours. This figure is the average estimated value of types of donated services, ranging from unskilled to professional.

The third and most accurate system compares each volunteer position to the equivalent staff position or the cost of the work in the marketplace. Take the per-hour wage figure and multiply it times the number of hours donated by a specific volunteer. Under this system, the work of volunteers performing clerical duties is valued at a lower monetary level than those managing major projects. You also can factor in the equivalent value of benefits that you don't have to provide for volunteers, such as insurance and vacation leave. In order to obtain a cost-benefit ratio, subtract the costs of operating the volunteer program. You can incorporate the proportion of time devoted by disbursed staff who supervise volunteers or devote time to related activities.

Evaluations, records, and value can be strong advocates for you. They provide tangibles, facts to prove the worth of volunteers. To implement these procedures effectively, you must use them regularly, accurately, and impartially.

7 COMMUNITY SERVICE VOLUNTEERS

Community service, also referred to as "court placements" or "compensatory time," is any volunteer work that is voluntary only insofar as the individual may select the agency in which he is placed. The worker is placed in an unpaid position with a nonprofit or tax–supported (governmental) agency to perform a specific number of hours in work or service within a given time.

Community service is usually ordered as restitution (in lieu of or in addition to incarceration, fines, and probation) for those who have broken a law. Time commitments may range from several hours to over five hundred. The average assignment is 24 hours.

Court-ordered community service workers can, and should be, viewed as another source to find volunteers. This large pool of people can provide your library with volunteers to help offset the volunteer shortage. This source, albeit unlikely, can have a positive effect for the library and the volunteer. The library receives a needed helping hand and the offender's rehabilitation may be enhanced by fostering social responsibility and improving self-esteem. However, as beneficial as a community service pool can be to a library's volunteer program, some agencies prefer not to take community service volunteers. The benefits and disadvantages, certainly, should be explored, before you begin, and even thereafter, on a regular basis, to evaluate the performance of this part of your volunteer program. Advantages and disadvantages of accepting community service volunteers are as follows:

Advantages:
1. Community service workers can be a regular, dependable source of volunteer assistance, particularly valuable for short-term, low-skill tasks.

2. Because the judicial system requires that hours be validated, community service workers may be more reliable than a new recruit.

3. Community service workers cover a variety of backgrounds and interests. If treated similarly to other staff and volunteers, they can become good-will ambassadors for your library. They also represent an immense pool of diverse talents.

Disadvantages
1. A certain amount of extra paperwork and procedures are required whenever dealing with any community service volunteers.

2. In order to comply with court specifications and to manage community service workers equitably, you must be absolutely clear

about your agency's requirements, work styles, and expectations that the workers will comply.

3. Because some staff may feel hesitation about working with community service placements, you must be equally clear with them about the types of infractions you accept, expectations about employees' behavior and procedures, and assurance of your full support.

THE BASICS OF OBTAINING COMMUNITY SERVICE

To initiate a relationship with a local justice system, try contacting the probation department, the police, or the courts. They will be able to tell you whom to call specifically and give you an overview of procedures and requirements. In most instances, you can limit referrals to certain types of infractions, ages, and numbers of hours. You should be able to screen applicants. Normally, offenders are interviewed by the judicial system regarding their interests, skills, and talents. If there is anything in a person's background that would pose a risk to your agency, this is supposed to be disclosed prior to making a referral. *Under No Circumstances Should You Be Or Feel Obligated To Take An Individual That You Think Is Unsuitable.* We never guarantee a placement at all; and the Denver Public Library is just one of a number of possibilities given to serve out the community service.

The easiest way to avoid potential problems before they happen is to decide, and get agreement from key staff, which types of infractions you're willing to use. At the Denver Public Library, we limit ourselves to persons with misdemeanors for the following categories:

- DUI — Driving under the influence
- DWUI — Driving with or under the influence of drugs
- NI — No insurance
- Traffic — Speeding/parking tickets
- Trespassing — In unlawful location—e.g., shopping mall violations (mainly students, 16 years and over)
- Fines — Traffic citations

Obviously no consideration is given to the idea of using people who might place our services in question—for example, persons charged with theft, larceny, embezzlement, child abuse, or harassment, or any felonies.

You should not create a volunteer opportunity simply to meet a potential community service worker's time constraints nor bend your *library's rules in other regards*. Courts give ample time to people to fulfill the most rigorous service or hours requirements. They also are usually amenable to modification if a true emergency occurs. Again, it is the community service volunteer's responsibility to manage time extensions or appeals to modify judgments, not yours.

Referrals are made directly from the court. It is the individual's responsibility to contact you in a timely fashion and ensure that all hours are registered, and paperwork is completed. Realistically, learning to take responsibility for their actions is important to community service volunteers. Some have a more difficult time understanding or complying than others. Obviously this lesson becomes even more crucial for these individuals' development.

When contact is made, paperwork must be received. Each judicial system—juvenile, city, county—usually has its own forms (see Figure 7-1 for sample form). By discussing the individual's needs, personal and court-ordered, and interests along with using interviews and screening similar to those for all volunteers, we refer community service workers to various offices or branches which may have a need for assistance.

Our In-Take Sheet summarizes the CS worker's basic information as well as the location of his assignment. It is the volunteer's responsibility to contact various locations and see if a match can be made. The volunteer then confirms placement with the Volunteer Office. Figure 7-2 is a sample of community service volunteers in-take sheet.

For community service people, hours of service must be accurately tracked and registered. Just in case a question arises, we require workers to sign in and out on a registration sheet that is kept in permanent records (See Figure 7-3). We also supply our own summary of completed work (See Figure 7-4) to supplement, complement, or take the place of court forms.

THE PROCESS

If you're new to use of CS volunteers, consider this process.

1. Carefully analyze if you can use these volunteers. They are a particular breed, and you must be able to adapt to them. Con-

106 RECRUITING AND MANAGING VOLUNTEERS IN LIBRARIES

FIGURE 7-1: Courtesy of Arapahoe County (Colorado) Judicial Services.

ARAPAHOE COUNTY COLORADO

JUDICIAL SERVICES

Alternative Services/Useful Public Services • Community Corrections • Pretrial Release Services

15400 E. 14th Place, #423	2009 W. Littleton Blvd.	7325 S. Potomac, #229
Aurora, CO 80011-5817	Littleton, CO 80120-2024	Englewood, CO 80112-4031
(303) 360-0172	(303) 730-1903	(303) 790-7201

MONITOR FORM

Participant's Name: _____   Case#:_____

TO BE COMPLETED BY AGENCY SUPERVISOR

Date	Time In	Out	Hours Worked

Date	Time In	Out	Hours Worked

TOTAL HOURS WORKED_____

DUTIES PERFORMED/AGENCY COMMENTS (IF THE PARTICIPANT'S TALENTS OR EXPERTISE WERE UTILIZED PLEASE DESCRIBE):

_____

_____

_____

_____   _____
Signature of Agency Representative   Agency Name

_____ / _____ / _____   _____
Date signed   Telephone

• •

PARTICIPANT'S COMMENTS:_____

_____

PLEASE HAVE PARTICIPANT RETURN FIRST PAGE OF THIS DOCUMENT BY _____ / _____ / _____

TO ATTENTION OF: _____

| WHITE: Alt. Serv. | CANARY: Agency | PINK: Participant |

FIGURE 7-2: Community Service Volunteers In-Take Sheet

VOLUNTEER SERVICES

COMMUNITY SERVICE VOLUNTEERS IN-TAKE SHEET

NAME _____

HOURS DUE _____ TO BE COMPLETED BY _____

HOME ADDRESS _____

CITY/ZIP _____ TRANSPORTATION _____

PHONE _____ (WORK) _____

DAYS/HOURS AVAILABLE _____

STARTING DATE _____ FINISHED DATE _____

ASSIGNED TO:

    LAC   ACCT, BLDG, CDO, CS, FRIENDS, HR, MKT, MP, PS, PR, P/DO, SUPPLY, VOL,

    BRANCHES ATH, BAR, BDY, BVL BYR, CRK, DAL, DKR, FIE, FOR, FPT, HAD, HMP, MCL, MLO, NC, PKH, SML, STORAGE, UNH, VVI, WDB, WES

    CENTRAL BSG, CHL, CIR/REG, HUM, ILL, MAG/COP, SOC/GEN, WHC

SUPERVISOR _____

VOLUNTEERS ARE RESPONSIBLE FOR KEEPING TRACK OF THEIR HOURS; MAKE SURE THEY SIGN IN AND OUT. VOLUNTEERS SHOULD ALSO KEEP HOURS AS ASSIGNED.

Please return this form *with* sign-in sheet *and* any additional paperwork to the Volunteer Services Office at LAC when the volunteer has completed the hours required. If you have any questions, please call Terry Nelson, 640-8957.

THANK YOU.

_____

(for office use only)

    CHARGE (DUI, DWUI, NI, TRAFFIC, TRESPASSING, FINES)

_____ COUNTY _____

FIGURE 7-3: Volunteer Sign-Up Sheet

Denver Public Library

ORIGINATING BRANCH/DEPT: _____

VOLUNTEER SIGN-UP SHEET
PLEASE PRINT

DATE	TIME IN	NAME OF VOLUNTEER	ACTIVITY	TIME OUT	TOTAL TIME

sider using CS volunteers only if you have work that is short-term, easily changed in terms of hours or types of duties, can be scheduled to meet the worker's time constraints, AND if you have in place a system for tracking hours as well as two supervisory levels—the first, on-site; the second, able to pull accurate reports on hours and activities upon demand (less than four hours).

2. Contact the local judicial system and determine their requirements for CS placements. When possible, obtain copies of their forms, guidelines, and requirements. They may require return of their forms within a certain period of time or on a particular document. Make sure that you can comply with these.

3. Survey or meet with your staff to determine their comfort level in working with CS placements and if they have the amount *and* type of work to justify regular contacts. Ask them to estimate the numbers of hours and/or people they may need over the period of a month or several months.

4. Prepare an initial plan and procedures. Don't forget standardized forms and information such as "Community Service Job Description" (See Figure 7-5) that summarizes your requirements for participation.

5. Appoint a primary contact (usually the volunteer director) and at least one secondary contact who will handle all initial interactions with judicial systems and all volunteers. They must be able to generate accurate reports upon request if necessary, and all placements must be registered with them.

6. Contact the judicial system and set an appointment. Ask them to give you sample forms and brief you about their requirements. Make sure you have the name(s) and phone number(s) of your primary contact—the person with whom you'll interact. Underscore that you are the liaison between your library and the justice system.

7. Decide if you and your library can benefit from, as well as assist, the judicial system by accepting community service volunteers.

8. Develop a record-keeping method for reporting hours, and for summarizing annual statistics. That way, you won't be caught unaware.

9. Initiate your community service activity, making sure that you evaluate it regularly. *All records should be kept a minimum of three years,* longer if your local judicial system so requires.

STAFF NEEDS

In order to utilize community service volunteers properly, you must have supervisors willing to work with court placements. Those supervisors on staff who are willing to do so should be identified

FIGURE 7-4: Community Service Authorization Form

Denver Public Library

1330 FOX STREET, DENVER, COLORADO 80204-2602

COMMUNITY SERVICE AUTHORIZATION

MEMO

DATE:

TO:

FROM:

RE: **COMMUNITY SERVICE HOURS**

This is to certify that _____ completed

_____ hours of community service at the Denver Public Library.

If you have any questions please call Terry Nelson, Volunteer Services Manager, 640-8957.

FIGURE 7-5: Job Description

JOB DESCRIPTION—COMMUNITY SERVICE VOLUNTEER

WHO:
Community Service volunteers are individuals who are placed in an unpaid position with a non-profit or a tax-supported (governmental) agency to perform a specific number of hours of work or service within a given time.

General Statement of Duties
- Performs any short-term library project as assigned.
- Promotes a positive public image of the Denver Public Library through all contacts with staff.

Supervises:
None.

Examples of Duties:
- Mends books.
- Does general filing, typing, and data entry (if capable). Calls on reserved books.
- Straightens and shelves books. Sorts books.
- Does folding and mailing.
- Performs other library-related jobs as assigned.

Qualifications:
- Meets community service guidelines as determined by the courts.
- Completes intake interview.
- Has proper paperwork.
- Reads and signs Community Service Worker Agreement sheet.
- Has one of the following infractions:

DUI:	Driving under the influence
DWUI:	Driving with or under the influence of drugs
NI:	No insurance
Traffic:	Speeding/parking tickets
Trespassing:	In unlawful location. Example: Shopping mall viotions (mainly students, 16 y and over).
Fines:	Traffic citations.

Time frame:
Completes assigned court-ordered ho

Supervisor:
Volunteer Services Manager, branch Central Departmental supervisor

prior to a program's enactment. These supervisors, in turn, should become the focus when dealing with community service volunteers.

When initiating a new program, start by scheduling a staff orientation for those who will supervise. Familiarize them with the types of court forms. Brief them about the categories of infractions you'll accept and your process for making assignments. Emphasize the necessity of correct reporting, especially exact number of hours. When a particular location or office is using as many community service volunteers as it needs, the staff supervisor should contact the volunteer director. This makes it all the more essential to build a rapport with staff supervisors so they feel comfortable reporting this.

If a problem occurs with a community service placement, and the staff supervisor or other employees feel uncomfortable resolving it, they should be advised to contact the director of volunteers. With this type of challenge, you can first try to reschedule the volunteer at another site. If behavior has been inappropriate or the volunteer unreliable, you may want to dismiss the individual immediately. It is better to have a formal dismissal system. The director of volunteers (or his representative) must be the one to dismiss the volunteer, contact the judicial system, or handle the matter in the appropriate fashion. Only he has the legal authority and responsibility to do so.

VOLUNTEER NEEDS

In exchange for providing the opportunity for constructive community service, volunteers hope for certain conditions. One is a convenient location. We expedite community service by placing volunteers near home or work. Assignments are more convenient for the volunteers, therefore it increases the chances of them fulfilling their assignments.

Another condition is the opportunity to perform their duties. These individuals are working to fulfill conditions set by a court, not to receive further punishment or condemnation from library staff. If the volunteer has any special skills, try to take advantage of these. They will improve your agency and at the same time they make the volunteer's experience more fulfilling.

When you are dealing with community service placements, remember that all records must be available not only to the courts but also to the volunteer. You should be willing and able always to provide the volunteer with a copy of what you've sent to the court.

The final stipulation is that you must be able to verify hours completed by any and all CS workers whenever a representative from a court requests. It is better to have more than one person who can track the time—for example, the volunteer director and staff person.

As instructions from a local court system say: *"When reporting work hours, you are providing legal testimony that your report is accurate. Warrants may be issued and people jailed based on the information that you provide . . . It is, therefore, crucial to have an accurate system of charting names, dates, and hours worked."* Figure 7-6 is an example of instructions provided by a court systems community service program.

ON THE JOB

Community service workers have some special needs and because their time commitment is definite and limited, orientation and training become compressed and adapted. You may find they don't need a full orientation, that an abbreviated overview of the library is adequate. However, you should still give community service workers a tour and make them feel welcome with a cup of coffee and a cheerful greeting, as well as a place to store their belongings, and introduce them to staff.

In terms of training, we find it useful to formalize the process by summarizing important points and procedures in writing. These are reviewed with the CS worker, and she signs the form to show she has read it. Figure 7-7 is an example of a community service worker agreement.

A FINAL, CRITICAL POINT

Libraries have a respected tradition of honoring the privacy of customers and staff. Although community service is entered on open court records, we strongly feel that an individual's selection of a library is his private decision. Just as our customers and staff have a right to privacy and confidentiality, so does the CS worker. Our role is not parent nor spouse nor judge. Our role is to provide the opportunity for the CS worker to fulfill his legal obligations in a manner to benefit him, the courts, and the library.

Community service volunteers share many duties. . .from simple to complex. Some examples of community service jobs are: building much needed bookcases, doing basic input into the computer database, special projects like folding and counting summer reading flyers for Children's Library, shelving books, filing, and mailings. Many of these tasks would go undone if it were not for the efforts of these useful public servants.

FIGURE 7-6: Program Guidelines Courtesy of Jefferson County (Colorado) Department of Corrections

Board of County Commissioners

Gary D. Laura
District No. 1

Betty J. Miller
District No. 2

John P. Stone
District No. 3

Dear Community Service Supervisor,

The following is just a reminder of our program guidelines.

You will receive a time sheet from our office. This time sheet indicates that the community service worker has been placed with your agency and is covered by medical insurance through our program.

❑ You should <u>not</u> allow anyone to perform any hours if you do not have a time sheet.

❑ Your agency is required to record all hours performed by the community service worker on the time sheet provided.

❑ The time sheet must be returned to the Jefferson County Community Service Program upon completion, or when the completion deadline has expired.

❑ Please have an authorized supervisor sign and date all time sheets whether or not all hours were completed.

❑ We also request that you keep a record of the hours worked by all community service workers after their service is terminated. This can be in the form of a copy of the Jeffco time sheet or another method of your preference. This is necessary in some situations in which we need to verify information.

❑ Any community service worker who works past his/her completion deadline will not be given credit for those hours and is no longer covered by our medical insurance.

❑ Any community service worker asking to work past his/her deadline should be instructed to contact their caseworker.

We appreciate all your efforts in utilizing community service workers and encourage you to call our office with any questions you might have. I can be reached at 233-4925.

Sincerely,

Ryan Ellis

Community Service Specialist

JEFFERSON COUNTY DEPARTMENT OF CORRECTIONS

Community Service
1667 Cole Blvd.
Building 19, Suite 350
Golden, CO 80401
233-4925

Director
900 Jefferson County Parkway, Suite 355
Golden, CO 80401
(303) 271-4840

Pretrial Services
1667 Cole Blvd.
Building 19, Suite 350
Golden, CO 80401
233-4421

FIGURE 7-7: Community Service Worker Agreement

COMMUNITY SERVICE WORKER AGREEMENT

Thank you for selecting to come to Denver Public Library. Your work here is greatly appreciated by our staff. Below you will find a few rules we ask you to follow.

While you are here:

1. Adhere to your work schedule. Many of your duties are arranged in advance of your arrival. If due to an unexpected emergency you are unable to come, please call the library as soon as possible.
2. Sign-in procedures: Be sure to sign in and out each day on the volunteer time record. In order for your hours to be accepted, a librarian or clerk must initial both the **in** and **out** boxes on your time record.
3. Telephone use: Please limit your telephone calls to emergencies only. Use the telephone in the work room and whenever possible, call out on the third line.
4. Breaks: Government law requires a minimum of a half hour lunch or dinner break (on your own time) for 8 hours you work. If you work less than 8 hours, the library requires a 15 minute break for a 4 hour work period. During the 15 minute breaks, it is required that you stay on library property unless special permission is given.
5. Kitchen and staff room use: Please feel free to use both the kitchen facilities and the staff room during breaks or your lunch/dinner time. Clean up thoroughly after you have finished eating.
6. Food/Drink/Smoking: Food and drink should only be consumed in the kitchen and the staff room. According to city law, all smoking must be done outside the building.
7. Dress: Since we are a public institution, you may have customer contact. Please dress accordingly. No halters or short shorts.
8. Radio use: Please do not use radios while the library is open except in the staff room and the basement. Keep the radio volume at a reasonable level so it will not disturb other library employees.
9. **Anyone** arriving for volunteer duty apparently under the influence of drugs or alcohol will be **immediately dismissed.**

Most of the time, you will be given a specific task to do. At times librarians and clerks will be busy and they will be unable to assign you a project immediately. If this happens, please proceed to the following list of self directed tasks *if* you have had prior instruction:

1. Shelve adult and children's paperbacks, jE's, audio cassettes, new books, magazines.
2. Straighten book shelves.
3. Make routing slips.
4. Call customers about recently arrived book requests.

Library work requires an attention to detail so your customers can easily find the materials they are seeking. Therefore, you need to do your job accurately. If you have *any* questions about the completion of your library projects, please question any available librarian, clerk, or shelver. Don't guess. We would like to emphasize the importance of following these guidelines, for failure to do so may result in your *not* getting credit for hours worked.

We appreciate your help and hope your time spent working at the library will be beneficial, productive, interesting and fun, too.

I have read the foregoing rules and agree to follow them.

Signature _____ Date _____

• Do you have a Denver County library card?   No_____   Yes_____

Although most CS workers are strictly temporary, the variety of their skills and interests is as diverse as that of the rest of the volunteer pool. Some of the more memorable have been:

- A highly respected member of the media whose CS work included giving us valuable advice on obtaining favorable news coverage.
- A young man who moved from CS worker, to volunteer, to paid staff over the period of several months.
- A very pregnant woman, grateful for a placement that allowed her to sit and be thrilled with the variety and challenge of her tasks.
- An articulate, charming woman who staffed and coordinated the library booth at a community festival over a three-day weekend, meeting the public with ease and enthusiasm about our agency.
- A strong-armed trucker with valuable skills and muscle power to put behind our movement of supplies and furniture from a huge convention hall in a short time.
- A computer programmer who custom-designed a program to track volunteer hours.

However as with all volunteers—and even staff—not every placement is perfect. We've struggled with community service workers who have arrived at the library under the apparent influence of alcohol or drugs—or haven't appeared at all—or carried a chip on their shoulders.

DISCRETION IS THE BETTER PART

Agency policies and guidelines are your best defense against problems because they state exactly what needs to be done. No pussyfooting around. Take a policy concerning alcohol and drugs. It presents procedures for dealing with the matter and the consequences that follow. Ours states: *Anyone arriving for volunteer duty apparently under the influence of drugs or alcohol will be immediately dismissed.* A more typical scenario is the CS worker who has neglected to arrange his schedule to allow adequate time for his service. This is not the agency's responsibility to rectify, even if "my mother will be angry," "my wife's been sick," or "my car broke down."

Sometimes a CS worker may lay claim to more hours than can be tracked through records. That's why your system for recording hours must be adhered to strictly. You do the CS worker a disservice if you fudge on his or her hours, or accept a placement for which you lack time and ability to supervise.

Rarely a CS placement doesn't "fit" at all. In this case, it is imperative that action be immediate and decisive, and that the individual be referred back to the court without delay. In one instance, a good-looking and apparently stable young man requested placement in a library setting. On the job he began making threatening telephone calls to his girlfriend. Fortunately, he was quickly dismissed from our environs. This cautionary tale seems so obvious that we hesitate to even mention it. But state it we must. It is a criminal offense for a community service volunteer to ask a worksite to sign off on hours in return for money or any other favor. It is also a crime to *accept* money or favors that might be construed as a bribe.

THE ULTIMATE VALUE

Our highest accolade came from a woman assigned to community service duty in a branch. She assisted with shelving and clerical duties, a placement we considered to be average, yet one she greatly appreciated. Afterwards she wrote a letter of thanks that she had been treated as a human being by staff, rather than "a piece of meat." What better result could we have asked for everyone involved? The individual benefited, and so did the library and our services.

8 THE R & R OF VOLUNTEERISM— REWARD AND RECOGNITION

"R & R" may stand for "rest and relaxation" in the military, but not for volunteers whose recreation consists of work and yet more work. Gluttons for punishment? Nonsense, they gain too much from volunteering to evaluate it by the same standards as paid employment.

Volunteering, as an activity on its own, has its own reward. Still we are all human, and we all enjoy a special glow that comes from knowing we've done well and from having our peers recognize the same fact. The large role that reward and recognition plays in a volunteer program makes the techniques for delivery equally important. We can give you a list of methods as long as your arm. None of them will mean a thing if you lack sincere appreciation. A solid gold plaque presented *pro forma* doesn't carry nearly the weight of a simple paper certificate that's given with heartfelt thanks and a hug.

Recognition of a volunteer's efforts is essential for a library to provide, because it helps retain the support of the individual for the institution, and to encourage the person's personal development. In order to demonstrate appreciation, the types of recognition must be as diverse as the people who comprise the volunteer corps. You've probably met some of them—the student preparing a project for independent study, the displaced homemaker sharpening her typing skills, the artist desiring a creative outlet, or the bibliophile wanting to spread the joy of books by hosting a guest author.

REWARDS FROM THE JOB

Many people take pride simply in completing the work assigned to them. These tasks might include collating a mailing or assisting a customer to find a book. Other volunteers prefer to create, own, and manage a project (see chapter 4, Assessment and Placement). Their satisfaction comes from putting their ideas into action, like the retired man who revitalized the DPL's delivery to the homebound; still another group may enjoy a very visible, public role.

Almost without exception, volunteers are seeking some sort of satisfaction not available in their regular jobs or routine lives. It might be participating in new experiences, developing skills, becoming part of a team effort, or socializing. It might even be total commitment to a worthy cause—the library.

Your purpose must be to provide a volunteer with a growth opportunity. The first step lies in discovering what would satisfy the volunteer, and then matching that volunteer with the appropriate task. The satisfaction that volunteers report in evaluations, the length of their service, the success of achievement, all corroborate the fact that the match was a good one. It is evident that the more comprehensive and accurate the initial screening and match, the higher the success rate in placements. Strange as it may seem, recognition sometimes equates with more responsibility and more work. Involvement of volunteers in planning, decision-making, and evaluation assures them that they are valued members of the library team. The DPL during its intense phase of construction and renovation of facilities had a number of citizen advisory committees which worked with staff, architects, and contractors. Library Friends groups frequently rely totally on volunteers to manage and conduct their activities.

TRAINING

An avenue sometimes overlooked is training. This can be structured to relate to hours or years of service, completion of projects, or selection for leadership. If your library presents training opportunities for staff—stress reduction, using computers, weeding techniques, customer service—you have a relatively easy task to reserve several spots for your volunteers. Broaden your choices by tapping workshops, seminars, and conferences sponsored by others in the community. The local United Way, churches, media, educational institutions, and organizations for directors of volunteers may host these opportunities at very reasonable fees. Library associations do the same with the bonus of a library perspective.

If your budget is flush, the ultimate reward is a free trip to a national convention. The American Library Association and related organizations welcome library volunteers at their conferences. Other professional associations and businesses related to library work do the same. Computer manufacturers, publishers, and fundraising experts are a few possibilities.

CAREER LADDERS

Rewards can be based successfully upon recognition of a volunteer's increasing skills and length of service by creating the equivalent of "career ladders." Winning the presidency of a group usually connotes an extra degree of confidence from the group's members. A promotion on the job shows appreciation for abilities. So an increase in responsibilities and supervision of others via an upgrade in title acknowledges a volunteer's outstanding work.

Think about creating a coordinator or manager for a group of volunteers who work at a particular branch; a shift captain during selected hours of a book sale; a volunteer chairman on a special project whose participants include staff as well as volunteers. An advancement may not necessarily constitute supervising others. Title changes can indicate proficiency or authority. Advanced storytellers might be called "masters" or beginning docents, "assistant docents." You can base promotions on the demonstration of skills or hours of service.

REWARDS AFTER THE JOB

Extend the life of your R & R efforts by incorporating items that survive after an activity or project is completed. For example, a letter of reference that you give to the volunteer to include in job applications, a standardized job description, and evaluation forms similar to those used for paid employment, can be retained in office files for permanent credentials.

Explore the possibility of a gift that keeps on giving. Certainly any volunteer with substantial hours donated should receive regular mailings of newsletters and announcements even after his commitment is completed. Figure 8-1 is a sample of the volunteer work experience form.

REWARDS ON THE JOB

Plain, common courtesy goes a long, long way. Simply treat volunteers the way you like to be treated. A word of thanks at the right time (or at an unexpected moment!) can make the cloudiest day seem cheery.

Other forms of instant gratification include small touches from a staff supervisor or co-worker—a piece of candy on the volunteer's desk, a get-well card, a birthday donut if that's standard procedure for your staff. Some offices like to feature their special helpers with an instant photo mounted on a bulletin board. The

FIGURE 8-1: Volunteer Work Experience Reference Form

VOLUNTEER WORK EXPERIENCE

Reference Form

Volunteer Name _____ Telephone _____

Address _____

City _____ Zip _____

Volunteer Job Title _____

Description of duties, responsibilities, tasks: _____

_____

_____

_____

Dates of service: From _____ To _____

Actual hours served in this volunteer job:

____ per day ____ per week ____ per month

_____ TOTAL

Training received: _____

_____

_____

_____

Comments: _____

_____

_____

_____

_____   _____
Signature of Volunteer   Signature of Volunteer Manager

Date: _____

NOTE: This certification is your record of volunteer experience. It should be retained as verification for future job reference.

FIGURE 8-2: Performance Rating Sheet

How's your on-the-job performance? Ask yourself the following:

Yes   No

____ ____   Regular volunteers receive the staff newsletter.

____ ____   Each volunteer has a special place of his own to leave files, receive messages, store belongings.

____ ____   You know your volunteers' birthdays along with those of your employees/co-workers.

____ ____   You took a lunch break/coffee break/after-work drink with your volunteers within the last six months.

____ ____   You have your volunteers' home telephone numbers in case of an emergency closing or bad weather.

____ ____   A volunteer sometimes gets so excited about an idea or a project that his enthusiasm rubs off on you.

____ ____   You know the approximate schedules of your volunteers without looking them up on a list.

____ ____   You greeted or said goodbye to every volunteer in your office that you saw this week.

____ ____   A volunteer made a suggestion to change a procedure in the recent past, and you accepted and implemented it.

____ ____   There's at least one volunteer in your office who works with no other staff around part of the time.

---

annual Volunteer Week (usually the third week of April) makes a perfect excuse to spotlight your particular group of volunteers.

Staff training cannot be neglected when recognizing volunteers. The staff supervisor should make a conscious effort to spend time with all volunteers, greeting them on arrival, thanking them when they leave, and including volunteers in staff activities. Figure 8-2 is a checklist to help you take stock of your performance with volunteers.

If you've got seven or more "yes" answers, you're probably as good at supervising volunteers as you are at doing the rest of your job. The previous list offers some guidance in the atmosphere that encourages the best efforts of volunteers. Note that respect for the individual, equitable treatment with paid staff, and freedom to function independently and with responsibility are as important as common courtesy.

Different offices have distinctive tones and customs. If yours is one that tends to be formal, a handshake in your place is the equivalent of several pats on the back at a more exuberant location. Don't worry about it. Just do what feels right. For you, that may be a formal thank-you card signed by staff—a special name tag—mention of a volunteer's efforts at the weekly staff meeting.

Do you verge on the corny? Try some of the more unusual variations of R & R, like the off-beat certificates shown in Figures 8-3 to 8-6. Other zany ideas could involve a huge piece of wrapping paper with a thank-you note signed by the crew, or a home-grown video birthday greeting rewriting the lyrics of a song to give voice to your appreciation.

FIGURE 8-3: Certificate Courtesy of the Association for Volunteer Administration, Pacific-Northwest Region X, Portland, OR, CLIP 'N COPY

The Up and Coming Award

Presented to

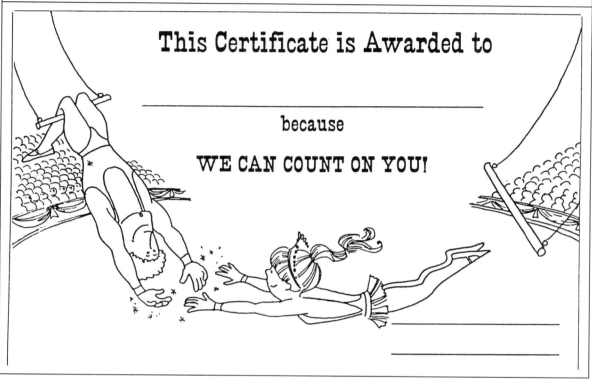

FIGURE 8-4: Certificate Courtesy of the Association for Volunteer Administration, Pacific-Northwest Region X, Portland, OR, CLIP 'N COPY.

FIGURE 8-5: Certificate Courtesy of the Association for Volunteer Administration, Pacific-Northwest Region X, Portland, OR, CLIP 'N COPY.

FIGURE 8-6: Certificate Courtesy of the Association for Volunteer Administration, Pacific-Northwest Region X, Portland, OR, CLIP 'N COPY.

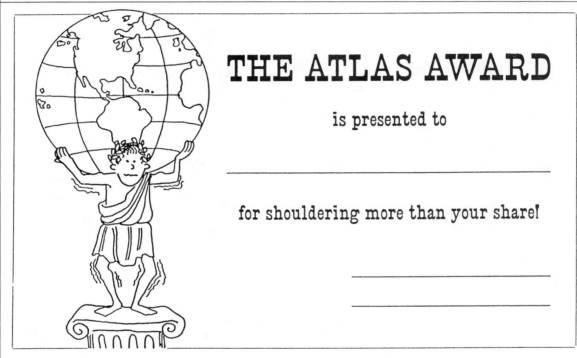

FORMAL RECOGNITION

Formal recognition methods permit the volunteer director to standardize certain responses, thereby guaranteeing that the entire library becomes aware of the importance of volunteers. They take up the slack just in case one office/branch/project forgets to show adequate appreciation. And they enable the volunteer director to capture a snapshot of the entire volunteer picture regularly to evaluate R & R. Formal R & R usually rests on two basics:

1. written acknowledgment of service;
2. a celebration.

The annual Volunteer Week provides you with the perfect excuse for some sort of recognition, or you can choose your own dates. A celebration involves both staff and volunteers and can be as large or small as you wish. You can use this time to schedule a lunch, ceremony, or party and even distribute certificates noting years of service. What about some of the following ideas?

- Posters distributed system-wide noting the celebration.
- Special buttons that identify volunteers during "their" week.
- Photo collages of volunteers and activities.
- A flower or balloon to each volunteer.
- A computer-generated banner with a message or names, surrounded by crepe paper.

CERTIFICATES

Certificates can be used in many ways. They are low cost, but tangible. You can create custom-made types for special events or particular types of duties; you can use them for the nominees of awards. Gorgeous versions, even bordered with gold, can be purchased at stationery stores and completed as you want. You can borrow designs from clip-art books or follow instructions on many personal computers or word processors. Figure 8-7 is an example of a ready-made certificate.

In ascending order of price and impressiveness are framed certificates, plaques, engravings, trophies, and the like. Some institutions have a permanent plaque on which names of various volunteers can be inserted as the years pass.

When you have set the accolades format, you need to decide on a vehicle for presentation. They can be sent through the mail, but many libraries like to feature the presentations at an event. The size and scope depend upon your energy and budget. The first consideration is scheduling. If most of your volunteers work at regular jobs during the day, there isn't any point in hosting a party during business hours. Lots of senior volunteers? Avoid night functions; a breakfast or lunch might be surprisingly popular with everyone.

DENVER PUBLIC LIBRARY
VOLUNTEER APPRECIATION RECEPTION

The Denver Public Library held a typical volunteer appreciation event for staff and volunteers. The invitation, sent to some 750 volunteers, asked people to gather on a weekday with staff right after business hours, from 5:30 to 7:30 p.m. The event was hosted at the Governor's Mansion—a location that many would like to see but wouldn't otherwise. As guests entered, they were greeted by several staff members who asked them to sign the registry and take name tags.

FIGURE 8-7: Certificate Courtesy of Association for Volunteer Administration, Pacific Northwest Region X, Portland, OR, CLIP 'N COPY

People should have no reason to feel intimidated. This is not a stuffy event. People can, and do, wander freely to sample the hors d'oeuvres and chat. Guests might admire the centerpieces and exclaim over a display of photos of volunteers in action. At about 6:30, the formal program should begin. At the front of the marble-floored hall, a guest speaker—this year the popular anchor of a television news show—speaks briefly on the importance of volunteers to Denver's quality of life. The City Librarian, Library Commission President, and President of the Friends also comment briefly but eloquently about the numbers and types of volunteers.

These leaders take turns presenting various awards: years of service, youth award, media award, docent, and nominees for volunteer of the year. Each volunteer gets a certificate. Finally, the evening's highlight—Volunteer-of-the-Year is announced. Gifts are presented to the winner—a complimentary suite at a local hotel, dinner for two, and a framed certificate. (See Figures 8-8 and 8-9)

With warm farewells and a small gift of appreciation for each person—this year an embossed pen—the volunteers leave. Total cost of the event and gifts—about $750. Total warm fuzzies felt by staff and volunteers—innumerable.

Here's a checklist of items to be resolved for any appreciation event:

_____ Date, time
_____ Location suitable for type of event
_____ Type of event
_____ Invitations
_____ Entertainment/speaker
_____ Master of ceremonies
_____ Schedule/agenda
_____ Program, other printing needs
_____ Refreshments, perhaps caterer
_____ Decorations, flowers
_____ Hosts, ushers
_____ Available parking
_____ Transportation (a nice touch can be car pools)
_____ Equipment, supplies (including name tags, microphone, podium, coat rack)
_____ Certificates, gifts, trophies
_____ Other items required by law or policy, such as security, licenses, first aid

**FIGURE 8-8: Reward and Recognition:
Youth Volunteer of the Year receive congratulations**

**FIGURE 8-9: Reward and Recognitions:
Dual winners of Volunteers-of-the-Year hold their plaques**

SPECIAL EVENT VOLUNTEERS

Special event volunteers are more difficult to treat like "family" because they come and go quickly for events and short-term projects. They require a different approach for recognition. Immediate, tangible rewards are great—for example, entry to an appearance by a famous author for volunteer ushers, a discount coupon to purchase used books for volunteer sales staff. Of course, thank-you notes or certificates of appreciation are always integral to the routine.

Special event volunteers deserve the same recognition as other people. Frequently they are the backbone of a library's participation in events like festivals and conferences. They sometimes become so interested in the institution that they will extend their commitment. Because they often volunteer in groups, they also are a conduit into corporations and other organizations.

INFORMAL RECOGNITION

Some R & R methods are a real treat and can be used for any type of volunteer. Through networks with community organizations and businesses, you can build up contacts for complimentary tickets to movie previews, admission to festivals or amusement parks, or tee-shirts to distribute to volunteers. Cooperative promotions really pay off in this regard. For several years, the DPL's thank-you to volunteers at the annual used book sale was free admission to a preview of a new motion picture or a local theatrical production.

Some forms of recognition can be employed in particular circumstances. These can make a difference to a volunteer's personal and professional life. Civic involvement is important in the corporate world. What better form of recognition than to notify a volunteer's employer of his dedication to a worthwhile institution like the library? For groups of volunteers from a particular business, as well as individuals, you can send articles and photos to corporate newsletters of their employees in action.

People who volunteer as a group, either from a business or another nonprofit organization, enjoy being affiliated with that group. Recognition in this case should extend to the group. A credit line on a flyer or program, a display of a banner or sign, the corporation's tee-shirt or cap, all help advertise the good work of the organization.

A recognition technique that reaches right into a volunteer's home is the greeting card. If you choose an unusual holiday, say Valentine's Day, or are able to confirm birthdays, your appreciation message carries real impact.

PUBLIC ACKNOWLEDGMENT

The Media

Public acknowledgment includes the general media, too. Society columns spotlight volunteer leaders, and "good news" columns are outlets for especially significant volunteer work or awards. Other possibilities include neighborhood newspapers, special interest publications (targeted, for instance, to seniors), and church bulletins.

Scheduling a radio or television interview for a volunteer demonstrates his or her value to the library and at the same time, increases agency credibility. The following examples demonstrate how media coverage advanced the agency's exposure. An article and photo about a Spanish-surnamed docent in a Hispanic newspaper acknowledged a valuable contribution, and also served as a recruitment tool. A retired volunteer appeared on a radio show for seniors to discuss library services to that age group and coincidentally to be an example of volunteer opportunities.

Library Publications

Library publications also provide an outlet for volunteer recognition. Staff bulletins, Friends newsletters, annual reports, event programs, can all serve as conduits.

STAFF VOLUNTEERS

Staff volunteers form a special category and require a particular touch. Because of labor and fair employment laws, some libraries may prohibit employees from volunteering at all. Others, like the DPL, make the distinction between employment and volunteering absolutely clear. An employee must freely choose to volunteer and must participate during non-working hours. His or her work must not replace that of a paid staff member.

An employee's incentives are identical to any volunteer's self-satisfaction, creative outlet, or experience. The library's "Now Famous Book Clappers and Kazoo Band," a well known participant in parades, is comprised of staff volunteers. The Friends Foundation Bookworm, a costumed character that appears at festivals, fairs, and events, frequently is an employee's alter ego. Employee volunteers enjoy reading to community children and staffing a booth at a street fair.

Recognition for employee volunteers is similar in nature. It includes certificates of appreciation and thank-you notes, articles in the employee newsletter, nominations for Staff Volunteer of the Year, and invitations to special events.

Employees at the DPL are recognized not only for volunteering with library activities but also for their work in the general community. Serving as a Scout leader, helping to tutor students, stocking a food bank, all increase the library's visibility and informal contacts as well as being charitable acts in themselves.

In the end, plain common courtesy goes a long way. Treat volunteers the way you like to be treated. A fancy gift can't substitute for appreciation person-to-person, and awards don't replace a worthwhile cause. By planning and implementing a comprehensive R & R program, a library can help all volunteers realize the significance of their commitment.

9 ACADEMIC, SCHOOL, AND SPECIAL LIBRARIES

Academic, school, and special libraries share many of the same challenges and opportunities for volunteerism with public libraries, and yet they also possess some unique qualities. The primary condition for these agencies is that they are part of a larger unit—a school, college, business, or medical center for instance. Although this may simplify recruitment (volunteers frequently have an association with the larger organization so recruitment can be targeted through the organization) it also means that you have less control over budget and planning.

THE BUDGET AND PLANNING DILEMMA

Indeed, the most common complaints from library staff center around the budget and planning. Aggravated conditions related to funding, primarily small staffs filling multiple roles, lead to a frustrating spiral of low staff/no time/no volunteers and ultimately a useless volunteer program. Even if the library locates volunteers, it may lack the time to develop interesting work and projects, train volunteers to handle complex tasks, or to evaluate the program.

If you're the single, even part-time, employee of a school media center, you do the best you can. That means setting your own priorities, and weighing the advantages and disadvantages of involving volunteers in projects. What do you do if you represent a college library in the midst of turf battles between academic divisions, alumni, development, and volunteers? You do the best you can by positioning your library's needs and opportunities in the menu of choices for the institution as a whole.

RECRUITING FROM A TRANSIENT OR LIMITED POPULATION

With constraints of time and money, it becomes critical that you closely define jobs and desired skills. Identify your needs such that when they are supplied will impact your work environment in an immediate and positive fashion. Additionally, have a firm understanding of the particular type of person needed to successfully accomplish the expected tasks. This beforehand knowledge will save time and money. Compare these with the obvious needs and limitations of the volunteer pool. Students usually adhere to the academic year of nine months. Be aware that students graduate and leave town. Maybe your institution is far away from most of the population center. Again factor these restrictions into the formula.

Job descriptions and self-awareness in hand, you can now work with the people or offices who manage volunteers or with the volunteer pool. Some examples of situations for seeking out volunteers:

- The parent-teacher-student organization at your elementary school publishes a newsletter each month. They also have meetings for all parents, as well as gatherings for home room representatives. All these provide methods to recruit volunteers.
- You arrange a meeting with the director of volunteers at your medical center. Your job descriptions help him or her to match several people in the existing files to your needs.
- Students, faculty, and local alumni are the pool for academic libraries. You design activities for students that acknowledge their temporary status, while those for alumni build their pride in the institution. Faculty members and their spouses can be a mainstay. A Friends group offers them challenging work as well as an avenue for recognition within the academic community.

RECRUITMENT TECHNIQUES

The following success story illustrates recruitment techniques.

At Aurora Public Schools in Colorado, media center directors frequently give mothers of incoming kindergartners tours of the facilities. At the same time, they present volunteer opportunities. Although you can predict these mothers will stop assisting at the end of their children's terms at the elementary school, five or six years is a good stretch for any volunteer.

Jody Gehrig, Manager of Educational Resources for Denver Public Schools, suggests a similar strategy. On the first day of school she posted signs throughout the building inviting parents to drop by the Instructional Media Center for coffee and donuts. The temptation was irresistible, and parents learned firsthand of the importance of the library and at the same time were presented with opportunities to participate.

TRENDS

Trends in contemporary society make their impact on school and academic libraries. Librarians mention a shrinking number of parents who are available during the day and competition for "free time" for all people.

Stay-At-Home Parents

Flexibility, adaptability, and creativity help you solve these challenges. About 50% of mothers of young children still tend not to work full-time because their days are segmented by chores, naps, and babies. A few hours of volunteer work in the media center when their kindergartner is in school may tempt them with its complete change in atmosphere, particularly if you can accommodate an occasional toddler, too.

Senior Citzens

The stereotype of seniors sitting around playing cards is entirely unfounded. Your school district may have an office that places retiree volunteers, or a college's alumni office can fill the same role. You might want to consider striking out on your own to the local community center, senior center, or senior high rise. Post notices, talk to staff, mingle at a lunch. Maybe arrange for show-and-tell by bringing some bright readers with equally appealing picture books to entertain a group briefly at a meeting.

Students

Students comprise a captive audience at schools. If regulations don't prohibit their involvement, you can consider utilizing their help before and after school, and during free times. At the middle and high school, and college levels, students frequently can obtain class credit or structure an internship for their work—an additional incentive.

What is common to all these approaches? As Gehrig points out, they contain a new perspective on volunteers, their work, and accommodating their needs. Library staff must take the broad view. Can books be sent to a parent to repair in the evening? Perhaps a parent with two babies could type at home. A nearby business might let employees read stories on their lunch hours.

TRAINING

If you're part of a larger system, a separate office may also play a role in training. Take advantage of what's offered; sometimes a general orientation to the institution can be provided, often in a very professional way. A volunteer office for a hospital or museum frequently develops a video, printed materials, and instruction on standard procedures for the institution. The alumni office or volunteer office of a college or school district may do the same.

Even without these services, as part of a larger institution you have some additional responsibilities to that body. It is to your benefit, as well as the institution's, to ensure that your volunteers have a general and positive overview of your school district, college, or enterprise. You'll find that your volunteers have become advocates for you within the larger organization. For the larger organization out in the community, it makes volunteers worth far more than the value of their time. You'll need to play a major role in training volunteers for the specific duties they will handle in the library. Step back a minute and consider what you want volunteers to do and how you can get them to accomplish this. What is the easiest and the most effective?

One-on-one training is most frequently mentioned by non-public libraries because it takes almost no advance preparation. It is also most time-consuming, and library staff hesitate to devote hours of training to a succession of volunteers who sometimes disappear without warning. Is there a method to consolidate training? Segment it so a volunteer "earns" additional training for time spent on the job or have one volunteer teach another.

Perhaps you can start with written procedures for basic tasks (maybe these already exist for paid employees). Or select one a month, even one a year to write up. Trade written instructions with your peers or plan a training session that is school-district-wide.

One special library complained that its volunteers wanted more professional level training than it could provide. This is when you explore new avenues like sending an individual to workshops, encouraging him to enroll in classes, or arranging for an adult internship at a large library.

REWARD AND RECOGNITION

In the close-knit community of a school or college, recognition of volunteer efforts becomes more important than usual to keep the social waters smooth. Although you may have difficulty getting a large newspaper to run an article about your volunteers, you do have access to more immediate avenues of appreciation.

Methods of reward and recognition range from internal newsletters to special perks. Most schools, colleges, and businesses are receptive to printing short items about volunteers in their newsletters, particularly if you write the article. Bulletin boards inside the library and out can announce volunteer achievements (appoint a volunteer to design the announcement).

Tap into resources outside your library. According to Jan Novak, district media resource teacher for Colorado's Aurora Public Schools, public and private libraries join together in their Aurora Library Council. Every other year the group hosts a tea for volunteers from all libraries. She also encourages library staff throughout the school district to nominate volunteers for awards sponsored by a variety of organizations. Sometimes an activity or service right at hand can become a reward. For example:

- One medical library provides a free meal in the hospital cafeteria for every four hours of volunteer work.
- A large museum is able to host an elegant annual dinner for all volunteers, including those at its library.
- An academic library grants free library cards to its friends, when other members of the public must pay a charge.

However, keep in mind that recognition makes the biggest impact when delivered by people personally involved. Ditto for expressing your appreciation, using appropriate means discussed in Chapter 8: The R&R of Volunteerism — Reward and Recognition. A verbal thanks, a note, or a handshake carry immeasurable value.

THE IMPORTANCE OF PLANNING AND EVALUATION

Even if your ability to utilize volunteers is limited by time and money, you cannot afford to overlook planning and evaluation. Libraries that limit volunteers to mundane tasks because they "aren't able" to plan, discover that volunteers are difficult to recruit and don't stay around long. If evaluation is neglected, problems will seem perplexing to solve and new opportunities will be overlooked.

In an informal survey of school, special, and academic libraries, we found a revealing trend: libraries that had no, or few, volunteers frequently lacked job descriptions, training, evaluation, input from volunteers on the program, even non-computerized data and files. Although some libraries clearly are so specialized or restricted that they can't use volunteers, in a number of instances libraries seem to do everything in their power to discourage the effectiveness of volunteers.

The application of planning, evaluating, and other management methodology isn't necessarily a yardstick to measure your success, nor will it guarantee you volunteers. Some libraries happily juggle a wealth of volunteers and projects without ever analyzing or recording a thing. But if you aren't one of these folks that operate by fortunate instinct, don't hesitate to use forms, checklists, and other resources. To balance your constraints of time and money with the need to plan and evaluate, try simplifying some of the forms in this book or other resources. Use these aids and concentrate management activities into one or two short periods a year.

TURN NEGATIVES INTO POSITIVES

ENCOURAGE RELIABILITY

Problems, challenges, and criticisms dealing with use of volunteers are not unique to school and academic libraries; but they can seem to have a greater impact on your services.

One volunteer missing from the schedule of a large public library probably doesn't make a major impact. But this can have major repercussions at a small school library. To encourage reliability, try some of these tips:

- Be clear, verbally and in writing, about your expectations.
- Make sure the schedule meets the volunteer's needs as well as yours.
- Give the volunteer several methods to deal with anticipated absences, such as alternative numbers to call or substitute workers.
- Enforce your rules. After the first unexcused absence, talk to the volunteer, explain the impact of unreliability on the library's services and potential consequences on the volunteer's assignments. If a second unexcused absence occurs, reassign the volunteer to less critical duties.
- Assign an entire area of responsibility to the volunteer, one that carries work over from week to week unless she completes it. An example is notifying students of overdue books. If the volunteer doesn't come in to complete the duties on one day, the work rolls over until the next designated day.

BROADEN YOUR VIEW

Schools sometimes feel that they cannot use volunteers because positions in the library are reserved for work/study students or class-credit situations. If you've been laboring under this misconception, talk to other staff and administrators. Find out if you're functioning under actual policy or simply tradition. Even if your institution prohibits volunteers, you may be able to get the rules changed for good reasons. Maybe your library always has used volunteers only for circulation and repair of books. Take off those blinders, and let recruits know about the amazing variety of duties and projects that abound. Encourage them to come up with their own ideas. At one library, a retired man refused the traditional volunteer opportunities. However, he proposed to serve as a homework helper located in the library. The effort became a highly successful venture.

FOSTER LONGEVITY

Another concern frequently voiced by libraries in the education community is retention and the commitment of a volunteer to return over months, even years. In small institutions, choices of tasks are limited or college libraries may need to restrict access to materials or areas. So how do you keep volunteers on the job? Give them ownership of tasks and projects. In addition to freeing up your time, the process enables volunteers to structure schedules and work flow to fit their needs. Because results depend directly upon volunteers, they are likely to demonstrate an amazing level of responsibility.

UTILIZE THE POSITIVES

FUND-RAISING

Volunteers can be an excellent source for raising supplemental funds at schools and colleges. Whether formed into Friends organizations, part of the parent-teacher association, or functioning as an ad hoc committee, volunteers spearhead drives to purchase materials and equipment. The following examples show how parents rallied to make some money.

- At one school, an outdated book sparked a parent volunteer into action. The book mentioned was *When Man Walks on the Moon. . .* "Distraught at the lack of timeliness, the parent became the impetus to obtain a grant for intensive book-weeding and the purchasing of new volumes.
- At the University of Colorado, the library Friends group published the *Colorado Cookbook*. The book is full of favorite recipes and attractive to alumni and gourmets alike. The resource has gone into several printings and raised some $200,000 to date.
- Who can resist the lure of a computer? Certainly not parents, particularly if they've used them at work or if they want to ensure that their children have access. Parents often are the means to acquire library computers through bake sales, grants, or promotions with local businesses.

CHILDREN AS VOLUNTEERS

They are all around you in a school. Why not give them an opportunity to grow, keep them occupied, and reduce your never-ending list of work all at the same time? Turn children into volunteers by assigning them jobs appropriate to their ages and interests. Some kids will go along because they are so eager to learn. Others might be trouble—noise-makers that you need to distract with a new challenge. In either case, you'll need to adapt tasks to the needs of the children. Focus on short-term activities for their limited attention spans with a definite beginning and end that enable the youngsters to see the progress they make. You will also need to make yourself available for questions and supervision.

The advantages to children of volunteering are numerous. It gives them something fun that can directly impact their skills in the academic arena. The child who is considered peculiar or a maverick builds his or her self-esteem and may even find a compatriot. In many schools, libraries are the primary location of computers, which children adore. They become miniature instructors to other youngsters. In fact, children often approach their peers for help more readily than an adult. So you'll be improving your library's service by using young volunteers.

CAREER TRAINING

Brag about the advantages of volunteering to recruits, especially the job experience it provides. Many homemakers take a first step back into the work world in school libraries. Just as in public libraries, schools provide a safe environment to learn new skills, test personal resources, and practice with modern equipment. School librarians provide credible and current references, too. School after school relate with pride the numbers of volunteers who have moved into the ranks of paid employees. Many have stayed in the fields of library science or education.

THE MOTHER OF INVENTION

Necessity generates some of the most creative applications of volunteer activity in school, academic, and special libraries by recruiting volunteers to meet challenges. Are you worried about preparing work for volunteers to handle? Assign one the duty for the next person. Do you need challenges for a bored volunteer? Ask him or her to create his or her own projects. Are you fielding requests for professional-level training? Appoint a researcher to call the local library association and colleges for ideas.

This technique can be extended as far as time and energy allow. A volunteer can schedule other volunteers and serve as the point-person for absences. An experienced volunteer can be paired with an inexperienced for training purposes. Paid staff must remain in charge and responsible for the overall operation of the library. But by giving volunteers autonomy and focusing on results, not methods, you'll increase your own effectiveness.

PROJECTS AND IDEAS

Have fun with your volunteers! Brainstorm new projects or have them direct one of the following:

- Design artwork combined with information on bulletin boards to intrigue children with new or popular topics.
- Host an appreciation tea for school staff; introduce them to new books and materials.
- Appoint a retiree as a listener; sit him or her in a rocking chair, and encourage the children to read to that person.
- Read, and read, and read, books in English to English-As-a-Second-Language students.
- Start story hours for parents and preschoolers when they are waiting for older siblings.
- Encourage children to read by throwing "parties" for authors in the months of their birthdays. Tell youngsters that they need to read a certain number of books to qualify for an invitation.
- Build more support for the library by presenting early morning coffee hours for parents during which they see computer demonstrations.
- Organize older or college students into library orientation guides at the beginning of school terms. This is a great way for them to make social contacts and ease staff of doing that task.

NEVER TOO OLD TO LEARN

A final hint—trade brazenly on the mutual aid society that exists among your peers. Staff at comparable libraries might have job descriptions, recruitment materials, and training manuals that you can utilize with impunity. What is the reward for implementing a volunteer program in a school, academic, or special library? Volunteers offer a new perspective, enthusiasm, and support. They make an impossible job, possible.

10 TROUBLESHOOTING

Policies cannot fit every situation, and standardized forms sometimes don't ask the right questions. This chapter covers some sensitive, puzzling, or potentially disruptive situations that others have confronted and resolved. Learning about them and finding out how others have dealt with these problems might help you think on your feet in similar circumstances.

Try As We May, We Can't Get All Volunteers to Keep Track of Their Hours. We Don't Want to Nag, But What Else Can We Do? Don't nag. You will lose more in terms of good will than you'll gain in statistics. This situation is especially true of people who meet regularly—for example, members of a governing board or officers and chairmen. Their thoughts seem to be occupied with the matters before them, and they have never had hour-counting emphasized to them. You don't want to lose track. The easiest method is to estimate the number of hours at a given meeting multiplied by the number of people usually in attendance times the number of weeks or months the group gets together. This system also works for the people who volunteer on a regular schedule in a branch or office.

A Volunteer Who Is Extremely Active with Our Library Also Is Prominent in the Local Community. Lately He's Been Making Statements in Public and to the Media Which Are Controversial and May Put the Library in a Bad Light Indirectly. Should We Stop Him? And How? Regardless of the issue or position, your volunteer has the same rights of expression as any employee or other citizen. You can, however, request that he or she make absolutely clear that this is his or her personal opinion. The best way for that person to do this is not to mention your institution. Should it arise, he can stress that he is appearing as an individual, *expressing his or her personal opinions,* and not appearing as a library representative.

A Fluent Speaker of Russian Called to Volunteer His Services As a Translator, But We Have Nowhere to Use Him. We Hate to Lose Any Potential Help. What Should We Do to Get Him Interested and Active? Clearly here is a person with a strong desire to serve and the confidence to be conspicuous. Even if you can't use his skills as a translator right now, you might at some time. Try intriguing him with an overview of several projects that would put him in contact with people, perhaps events or services like bookmobile delivery. If these don't appeal to him, or if he tries them and decides against them, your best response is to help him find a volunteer placement where he can use his skills (remember collaboration?). Therefore, when you do need a translater of Russian, the pleasant feelings associated with your cooperative behavior will make the probability of your obtaining one much higher.

What Do You Do with a Volunteer Who Has "Roving Hands"? A situation such as this causes policies and procedures to face a serious and delicate test. Your library's standards for employee behavior should be equally applicable to non-paid workers. On a practical level, the problem of sexual harassment usually does not reach the dramatic proportions portrayed on television shows. Word-of-mouth, innuendo, or a raised eyebrow may be the hints. Also take note that volunteers won't feel comfortable to admitting a concern unless you have established an atmosphere of trust and confidentiality.

Track the rumors if you can, and then attack the problem at its root—the instigator. It's desirable to get advice from your agency's human resources director or attorney before you begin any action. Clearly define acceptable and unacceptable behavior. If standards are violated, you must dismiss the volunteer, otherwise you leave yourself open for legal action by victims. You also must ensure that you record your exact course of action, each step you take, or you are vulnerable to legal action from the alleged perpetrator.

Some of Our Top Management Insist That the Success of Our Volunteer Program Be Measured in Increases in Numbers of Hours and People. Consequently, the Emphasis Here Has Been on Recruitment, Recruitment, Recruitment. Are There Any Pitfalls to This Approach? You'd better believe it! Far worse than having no volunteers is having a surfeit. Note that we are not speaking of a *surplus;* anyone who's worked with volunteers knows that you must allow for attrition, illness, bad weather, or unreliability. Volunteers like to feel that their efforts are making a difference. How can they believe that they are having an impact if they twiddle their thumbs as part of an unoccupied herd? Or if they never even get placed because the frantic staff lacks time to schedule interviews?

Convincing management that quality is more important than quantity is a separate challenge. Try comparing the training, placement, and supervision of volunteers with that of employees. Most supervisors agree that certain resources are required to manage paid staff adequately. A second approach is to pinpoint the types of skills, backgrounds, schedules, and hours that volunteer tasks or projects require and discuss these with management. This may help them understand your selective recruitment techniques, and why quality is more important than quantity.

We Always Seem to Be Able to Attract New Volunteers, But They Never Stay. What Can Be Causing This Situation? We're Tired of Training People Who Leave Quickly. Several conditions may be affecting your retention rate. First, you must realize that no volunteer stays forever. People get jobs, move, have babies, go through other life changes. And volunteers have a high attrition rate. Your percentages may not differ radically from any other organization's. Check with volunteer directors outside your library to find out if you're experiencing particularly poor retention.

If this is not the case, two other areas make a major impact on volunteer satisfaction—placement and environment. The most common problem with placement has to do with assignments that are either too routine and simple-minded, or, at the other extreme—complex and challenging. Do you expect volunteers to stuff envelopes day after day, month after month, with no change, or shelve books like automatons? If these are representative of the only tasks that you give to volunteers, they are probably bored, and not feeling important to your operation.

On the other hand, perhaps you expect volunteers to perform beyond their comfort level by writing a newsletter article, organizing a book drive, or appearing as a speaker to a community group. Unless you carefully monitor volunteers as they try a new effort, you may discover them quietly slipping away. Solutions? Careful interviewing and placement, regular evaluations, pairing volunteers with an experienced and enthusiastic staff member or volunteer, and assuring people that they can approach you with concerns, and receive good advice and help.

If neither of these extremes applies, you're left with the environment. Are volunteers treated like interlopers or second-class citizens? Is a supervisor especially rigid or remote? Remember that most volunteers seek a social connection as well as worthwhile work. A clue that you have a problem with the work environment comes when volunteers consistently and persistently drop out of a placement at a particular office, branch, or activity. Training, reassignment of volunteers to a new supervisor, or a joint conflict resolution may help.

What Do You Do with a Volunteer Who Just Isn't Working Out? Pinpoint the cause, starting with confidential interviews with key staff, possibly continuing with direct observation. Is the problem lack of training? Conflicts with staff? Erratic attendance? One time we had a volunteer suspected of "tippling" before work, which caused her to duplicate and lose track of her own progress.

Address the concern in a private meeting with the volunteer. You need to delineate work performance, however, not theorize about motivation or drag in personal judgments. In addition to being counterproductive these may represent a violation of civil rights. Give the volunteer an opportunity to air his or her own perspective.

Many staff supervisors feel comfortable handling this process on their own, once they've alerted you to a potential problem. Others want you in charge. In either case, an evaluation must be made to decide if results justify the amount of time and resources necessary to resolve the situation. Find out if the volunteer, staff supervisor, and you can develop a solution. Reassign the volunteer to another position or task, or provide more training.

We'd Like to Use More People with Disabilities As Volunteers, but Truthfully, Some Staff Are Ill at Ease Working with Them. At the heart of the problem is the strangeness of the situation. As persons with disabilities become a familiar part of your library, you'll find staff loosening up. Periodic workshops on the topic will help give staff the volunteers' perspective and bring concerns to the surface where they can be discussed.

You can identify key employees who feel comfortable around people with disabilities for initial volunteer assignments. On your end, make an extra effort to match the volunteer with appropriate activities and offer encouragement. Another way to alleviate concerns is to make sure that the volunteer's emergency contacts are current and easily available to staff. Provide training to address specific hurdles—for example, methods to communicate with a volunteer who has both hearing and speaking impairments. As usual in any human relationship, an atmosphere of trust and frankness always helps.

What If a Volunteer Has an Accident or Medical Emergency? Just as with paid staff, you should be familiar with your agency's procedures. Some libraries require that you use a particular medical facility, and many ask that special forms be completed for the record. Also make sure that the all-important list of emergency contacts is current AND available immediately; and then, use it. The process is applicable for psychological emergencies as well. We tested our response system recently when a young woman at one of our libraries suddenly broke into an intense and persistent crying fit from emotional problems. Staff was able to reach a close relative to assist.

We're Desperately Short-Staffed and Really Could Use Volunteers to Handle Tasks Like Routine Filing and Typing. But We Can't Seem to Find Any. We're Frustrated! Step back a minute and view your situation. Are you trying to supplant paid employees with volunteers? This is a very controversial position. Staff begin to fear their own replacement by volunteers, and volunteers resent working for free when others get paid. Maybe you're just trying to deal with increases or changes at your library. You still need some perspective on your request. Are you lumping all of the boring, repetitive tasks together? Would YOU volunteer for this position? Try mixing in some challenges, like developing responses to suggestions for book purchases; or adding a social aspect, like assisting customers to find materials; furnishing responsibility for managing the schedule of telephone calls for reserved items.

Last, make sure that you are aware that clerical work is often the most difficult volunteer position to fill. In today's world, most women as well as men must draw a salary for work performed during business hours. Your best possibilities probably are retirees or people wishing to retrain for the job market.

We Have Some Concerns about Confidentiality in Regard to Volunteers. As library staff, we deal with issues about confidentiality every day. Naturally, volunteers should be instructed in your agency's policies, and those policies should be enforced equitably. For instance, the records of customers are not released without due legal process. A volunteer's violation of confidentiality should be handled just like an employee's.

Volunteers have a right to expect confidentiality from the institution, too. Home addresses, phone numbers, work schedules, and other personal information should not be revealed unless there is a very good reason. Individuals performing community service through the judicial system should have confidence that your staff will not broadcast their background.

The last area concerned with confidentiality is that amorphous atmosphere on the job. Volunteers welcome friendly chatter about marriages and births, and informal discussions concerning new projects or challenges; complaints and malicious gossip are inappropriate. Volunteers should not be required to bear the burdens of dissatisfied employees or be manipulated by staff for dubious ends. And you wouldn't want erroneous information or any critical discussion of personalities or procedures circulating in the community from a chatty volunteer.

We're Just Starting Our Volunteer Program. Where Can We Get Help? Ask the experts! Regardless of the size of your community, and even if every library in your area is a novice to volunteer management, many organizations utilize volunteers. Churches, hospitals, and youth groups have long, successful histories of management. Managers of volunteers, whether paid or unpaid themselves, usually are happy to give advice, suggestions, and examples. Sometimes these folks meet and explore other local organizations. Denver has one called the Business Volunteer Alliance, created to encourage volunteers from the business community.

Another option is formal training. As management of volunteers becomes more complex and specialized, a number of colleges and universities are offering classes, certificate programs, and even degrees. Professional organizations, such as Directors of Volunteers in Agencies (DOVIA) and the Association of Volunteer Administration (AVA), sponsor workshops, seminars, and conferences.

How Can We Inject Some New Enthusiasm and Energy into a Volunteer Program That Has Been Around for a While? Idea-swapping, back-slapping, and comrade-hugging are the best ways we know. And where do you get them? Often by meeting with other people in similar situations. Regional or local chapters of DOVIA and AVA hold regular meetings and support seminars and publications. Or you can start your own roundtable. In Denver, we formed a group called the Metro Libraries Volunteer Management Council several years ago to share information and support.

If these aren't available, try attending conferences on related topics such as marketing or management. Don't overlook your own staff and volunteers. Host an informal coffee hour with visionary conversation to dream about "what if's." Ask several people to read articles or chapters from volunteer-related publications and share thoughts at a brunch.

We Hate Even to Broach the Subject, But How Do You Fire a Volunteer? Very carefully—It's even more difficult than similar actions for paid employees because, after all, these folks are working out of the kindness of their hearts. You may laugh, thinking that you're so overwhelmed by recruitment and retention issues that a matter of termination is beyond comprehension. But whether from health problems, maladjustment, or inability to perform the tasks, sometimes a volunteer must be terminated.

Volunteers have been known to take their complaints to the media if dissatisfied with their dismissal. You don't want to wash dirty linen in public—or in court—so you'd better be able to substantiate your reasons.

As with other aspects of volunteer management, forethought and planning hold the keys to efficiency. They mitigate against the number and complexity of terminations. The process begins with a signed application form from the volunteer, a job description, performance appraisals, and permanent records in the volunteer's personnel file. Clear procedures, guidelines for absences and similar office matters, volunteer and supervisor handbooks, reasonable performance standards, formal orientation and training, all support fair practices that benefit volunteers as well as you and your agency. They also provide a source for objective evaluation of work.

Although criticism about performance may be initiated by staff as well as customers, employees frequently are reluctant to file a formal complaint that could result in dismissal. A problem-solving assessment form is shown in Figure 10-1 followed by a sequence of steps to objectify the procedure and further validate your actions.

The following list describes the steps you need to take when considering the termination of a volunteer. However, this could also be applicable to paid staff.

Steps include:

1. Meet with supervisor to determine concerns and possible solutions.
2. Meet with volunteer to relay concerns and possible solutions, focusing on desired behavior. Make sure that all items and responses are summarized in written form for your files.
3. Allow time and opportunity for the volunteer to improve. The supervisor should be involved in documenting behavior.
4. Final resolution of the matter with volunteer.

In some instances, this process may be too cumbersome. Suspected illness should be immediately brought to the attention of the volunteer's emergency contacts. If your volunteer policies address illegal drug use, you have grounds for immediate discharge in these instances. You also may discover alternatives to actual dismissal. Some options for termination are as follows:

> **FIGURE 10-1: Problem-Solving Assessment of Performance**
>
> PROBLEM-SOLVING ASSESSMENT OF PERFORMANCE
>
> 1. Does the volunteer comply with normal office procedures?
> 2. Is rate of absenteeism reasonable? How many assigned hours/days has the volunteer missed in the preceding month?
> 3. Does the volunteer have a regular job assignment? A written job description? Are there standards for work?
> 4. Is the volunteer meeting standards? If not, in what way is he deficient?
> 5. How does the volunteer relate to customers? To staff?
> 6. Are there health or safety concerns related to the volunteer?
> 7. Has the volunteer's behavior changed significantly recently? In what way?
> 8. Have conflicts between the volunteer and staff or customers increased? Have complaints?
> 9. What steps have been taken previously with the volunteer to attain improved conditions and production?
> 10. What alternatives exist to the current placement?
>
> Other comments and concerns: _____

- Reassignment of a volunteer to a different office or program.
- Retirement to an "emeritus" status, that enables the volunteer to serve in an advisory capacity.
- Restructuring of duties to those for which the volunteer is better suited.
- Referral to another nonprofit agency (in jargon, "outplacement").

We Want to Start a Volunteer Program Because We Really Need Help. But Then Someone Mentioned Insurance, Accidents, Risks to Library Staff and Property As Well As to Volunteers. Should We Worry about These Topics? We live in a litigious society, and certainly you should check with your legal advisor to determine if you need to take any specific action. You will probably discover that your library's current method of insurance covers nearly every possibility for volunteers, too. You may need to prepare some documents for specific occurrences, for example, incidents related to community service workers, and definitely to limit access to some equipment like vehicles or paper cutters. You DON'T want to let fear of legalities prevent you from operating a volunteer program. No one can guard against every possibility, and common sense goes far in preventing problems. By starting small, with manageable components, you'll be able to address concerns in a reasonable manner.

We Need a Large Group of Volunteers Several Times a Year—One Time for a Special Event, and Then As Story Readers. Do We Really Need to Bother with All That Minutiae about Orientation and Training? Let's be practical. Time, resources, and desired outcome affect how much training and orientation you can and should provide. One advantage of large groups of volunteers is that you can standardize your instruction. Try scheduling several sessions over the period of days or weeks from which recruits select. Or, depending on the event, you might have volunteers show up an hour early before their shifts. This is also where classifications help. Appoint several long-term volunteers as your assistants, shift captains, or some similar designation. They can teach, direct, coordinate, and serve as your second and third pairs of hands and heads.

However, we do suggest that you incorporate at least the basics of orientation regardless of the volunteers' assignments. By arming volunteers with fundamentals like a brief history of your library, management structure, hours, and upcoming events, you will create a group of advocates as well as workers.

We've Got So Much We Could Do, We Can't Decide Where to Start. Help! The process for moving from talk to action rests on a series of steps. It's often a good idea to initiate the process at a retreat or a time period of several hours during which no interruptions are permitted. You can invite volunteer office staff, key volunteers, other managers, staff supervisors, or whomever works for your library. The following steps are provided to give you a head start with your program.

1. Brainstorm challenges, issues, ideas. Include goals mandated by top management.
2. Group these into broad areas of concern, regardless of how eclectic. You'll find that some statements are problems, some contain answers, some are just letting off steam.
3. Try to re-state broad areas as general goals, such as "Get more volunteers" or "Have the volunteer program become more visible in the community."

4. Brainstorm objectives to reach the goals. Don't spend too much time on pros and cons for each objective at this step.
5. NOW assign values for characteristics like priority ranking —high, medium, low—time range to implement money and other resources required and staff responsibilities. You'll find precedence of one objective over another occurring almost spontaneously.
6. Assign objectives to key staff members. They become responsible for getting a group of folks together to refine each objective and develop an action plan—a set of steps to achieve the objective. (An unstated rule—people in each group should be involved in implementing the work, too.)
7. Meet regularly to chart progress and revise objectives. Figure 10-2 is an example of a planning process grid, that summarizes, condenses, and guides the entire operation.

We Have Very Active Labor Unions in This Area. Can They Affect Use of Volunteers? Yes, but a number of libraries with unions also have successful volunteer programs. Impact depends upon several factors: the year of the establishment of a union and volunteer program; resources that are available; and communication between the union and the library. Libraries that have unions should discuss the volunteer program with leaders before initiating or expanding it. Careful definition of jobs and duties for paid staff and volunteers can eliminate many potential disagreements. In general, if a job description exists for a paid position, or if work requires library professional training, a volunteer probably should not be used.

It might be helpful to structure and or redefine a Friends organization to manage most, if not all, volunteer activity. Various duties can be assigned right from the beginning either to paid staff or Friends volunteers. Friends can direct special events, community outreach, and public relations for themselves on behalf of the library.

You Talk about Establishing an Atmosphere of Trust and Confidence in the Volunteer Program Director. What Do You Mean, and How Can We Achieve This? "Trust" means several things. First, that volunteers and staff feel comfortable asking questions and making mistakes. We are not suggesting that you set low standards nor that you accept sloppy work and carelessness. But if individuals fear that they will be called on the carpet for honest errors, they naturally hesitate to try any new activities or welcome innovative situations. They balk at performing any tasks outside

FIGURE 10-2: Planning Process Grid

(Shows possible objectives for a volunteer program.)

Objective	Priority	Range	When	Who	Resources	Status
Plan staff workshop	High	Short	9/93	TN	$150	In progress
Write staff manual	High	Medium	3/94	BC	Paper, printer, $250	Start 12/93
Rent video on service	Medium	Short	9/93	MS	$10	In progress
Design R & R award	High	Short	9/93	TN	$25, two hours design	Start 8/93
Buy prizes	Low	Long	6/94	VR	$500	Review 10/93
Prepare written quiz	Medium	Medium	1/94	TN	Six hours	In progress

their immediate job descriptions, and morale plummets. The following list describes what you should do when this occurs.

- **FOCUS ON THE POSITIVE:** Were reasonable results achieved? Did people attend a lecture even if the refreshments never showed up? Was data entered on a computer despite a volunteer's erratic attendance record? Stress the good, even if you have to say, *"Well, we've learned from experience not to try THAT again."*

- **EVALUATE OBJECTIVELY:** When you and others review an activity, a project, or a person's performance, do so without making personal remarks or placing blame. Try asking *"What went right and what can be improved?"* or *"Did we achieve our goals?"*
- **ENCOURAGE THESE ATTITUDES IN STAFF SUPERVISORS:** All of your good work will be undone if those who work side-by-side with the volunteers demonstrate negativity and constant criticism.

Second, trust also conveys elements of confidentiality and availability. Your policy for general contact must be to keep your office door and telephone line open as much as possible, even without a scheduled appointment. Comments and suggestions that people make should not be revealed to others without their consent. Naturally, you allow for subjectivity and emotion, and you do not react to negative statements without substantiating them.

Last, trust includes actively encouraging suggestions about the volunteer program. You do not become defensive when people give you advice or comment about success or failure of an effort or individual. You begin this with regular, formal evaluations (see Chapter 6, Evaluations and Records). Continue by being receptive to casual conversations, asking for ideas, and welcoming interaction.

Trust does not occur overnight. You must earn it, with your own integrity and fairness, individual by individual, and incident by incident. It is a never-ending process that pays off in an outstanding volunteer program that your entire library supports.

11 TYPES OF VOLUNTEER PROGRAMS

Volunteer programs vary as widely as volunteers themselves. Although some may be "typical" around libraries, others are unusual enough to be mentioned for the new horizons they will open to librarians and to volunteers. Still, others demonstrate particular skills or traits that you may wish to encourage.

One item to keep in mind is that you gain diversity in types of volunteers by encouraging a diversity in staff supervisors and a concomitant diversity in assignments. Diversity of customers often follows. Although this phenomena has long been noted in situations with paid employees and their managers, its application is rare in many situations utilizing volunteers. A volunteer is a volunteer, right? Someone who puts in five to ten hours a shift. Wrong.

A branch manager who stresses procedures and details usually values the same in her staff and volunteers. An individualist might have trouble adjusting to the routine. A department where employees of all levels function independently probably will have a low tolerance for volunteers who need to be supervised closely. So you see that staff members who select the volunteers tend to choose people who fit into the existing situation.

We are not making a value judgment about which type of management style is best. That depends upon the responsibilities of the project or activity as well as the personalities involved. We are suggesting that the easiest route to the utilization of a variety of volunteers is the encouragement of staff supervisors of volunteers who have a variety of personnel techniques. This way you have the best of all possible worlds.

STAFF AIDE

Sometimes the most mundane tasks assume a real appeal if you group them together and focus on their true responsibilities and goals. After all, doesn't every job have its tedious elements? Staff aides often are the glue that holds together staff in moments of extreme pressure or stress. If you convey the importance of this role, plus the variety of tasks inherent in it, and the affiliation with the library's staff, the recruitment of dependable volunteers committed to service delivery should be straightforward.

"Staff aide" is a general category for support activities. Individuals capable of a great deal of autonomy and personal accountability are especially suited to the position, particularly if they can work

FIGURE 11-1: Dependable help in the office is often difficult to locate. Retirees, like Claudia Deming, are one source.

alone. Staff aides assist staff members with clerical tasks, basic research, circulation activities, computer and audio-visual usage, and materials repair. They also can help with typing, word processing, photocopying, alphabetizing, filing, shelf reading, and other general clerical projects.

A staff aide should be qualified to perform basic clerical skills, be willing to help and to learn new skills, be open to new ideas and experiences, along with the ability to work effectively with a diverse public and staff. As with many volunteer positions, if you can assign the staff aide with a regular schedule, you will stand a better chance of retaining that person long-term. Genuine interest and involvement in the job are great motivations to stay.

SPECIAL PROJECTS

For an all-round specialist (if there is such a thing), consider the Special Projects volunteer. This individual has particular skills you'll want to use; or, vice versa, he wants to participate in volunteering

FIGURE 11-2: Volunteers index files and materials in the Western History Department, expanding services to all customers.

in very specific ways. Maybe you hope to tap local writers, artists, speakers, academicians, or bibliophiles. Perhaps you need help with an annual library card registration drive. Then you want to recruit for special projects volunteers. These people can assist with displays, archives research or organization, graphics, oral histories, community festivals, book-sorting, speaker's bureau, read-alouds, special collections development or maintenance, and community outreach.

They must be willing to take training necessary to perform duties of special projects (e.g., read-aloud training, speaker's bureau training). They should also be able to make a commitment for a certain amount of time sufficient to complete tasks. This means that you should be able to estimate the amount of time and type of training, along with the people who will provide the training.

Although they work under the direction of an employee, special projects volunteers often must function on their own for long periods of time. This means they need to possess initiative, personal responsibility, and excellent decision-making judgment as well as particular skills.

Recruitment for special projects volunteers is most successful when it's word-of-mouth, perhaps contacting a person who has been recommended, or approaching a group whose members exhibit the interests you're trying to tap — a writers' organization, a professional accounting association.

DOCENTS

Docents (from the Latin word "to teach") are highly skilled volunteers, trained to perform special projects, who make a long-term time commitment. At the DPL, docents handle tasks like helping customers use the Library's CARL computer system or staffing regular read-alouds for children, leading tours of facilities, and answering customer questions at the information desk.

Docents are expected to complete an intensive docent training program, maintain membership in the Friends Foundation, and commit one year (after training) to the DPL Docent Program. On the benefits side, docents deepen their knowledge of library collections and learn valuable new skills in teaching, community service, and computer technology. The difference between docents and "regular" volunteers is based on the depth of their formal training, the nature of their responsibilities, and their specific time commitment.

HOMEBOUND SERVICE

One of the most popular volunteer programs throughout the nation is service to the homebound. Homebound volunteers deliver library materials to people who are unable to travel to the library or who are highly restricted in their travel — usually seniors or persons with disabilities. Dedicated and caring individuals who possess great sensitivity and patience make the best homebound volunteers. Because they function without direct supervision and interact with vulnerable people, homebound volunteers for the DPL must first complete a Criminal Bureau of Investigation check as well as the volunteer skills form. After these preliminary stages are completed they will receive a homebound training packet to review. Finally, volunteers are matched with a homebound customer, usually based on geographic convenience.

After arranging an initial meeting in the homebound customer's residence at their mutual convenience, the volunteer selects material from the library. The volunteer uses resources like the computerized catalog, lists of large-print books and books-on-tape, and the

FIGURE 11-3: A self-supervised volunteer works on a map project.

customer's personal preferences to get an idea of acceptable materials. He may assist the homebound customer to obtain a library card if needed. When items are due or the customer is finished, the volunteer returns materials.

Homebound volunteers work approximately three hours every six weeks. They are asked to commit to six months of service at a time.

STUDENT INTERNS

One of the best sources for energetic, enthusiastic, and bright volunteers is the local school system. Like other volunteers, interns come in all varieties. Their key motivator is obtaining experience to fulfill whatever academic or personal requirements they may have.

Many library schools require internships or practicums. These students may have as many on-the-job library skills as a paid employee. But your search for interns can go much farther than the logical choice of library school. Begin your recruitment at the high school level. Your school district might have a special program for gifted and talented teens or a work-for-class-credit effort. For example Atlanta public schools require all students to complete 75 hours of community service. A call to administration headquarters should give you an indication. An alternative is to talk to the librarian or English teacher at the local high school. They may have suggestions or be willing to provide extra credit to student volunteers. A federally funded program called Youth Service Learning exists in some schools. This effort with a vocational slant stresses practical on-the-job exposure to accustom students to a work setting and accompanying work ethic.

There are many intern programs at the college level. Your proposal will be in competition with many others, including paid positions, so you should make the internship sound as attractive as possible. Stress the variety of experience needed, the level of responsibility, and the importance of tasks. Internships can be skewed in a number of directions, depending upon your needs and the student's major. Don't limit yourself to students in library and information science or English. Include majors like journalism, marketing, communications, business, finance, education, and computer science. These majors and many others lend themselves to work in libraries, because they encompass all types of interests.

Interns versus Volunteers

The following list provides the characteristics which distinguish an intern from volunteer work.

1. It involves a student, recent student or trainee in a formalized structure.
2. It has a definite beginning and end with a particular number of hours per day or week to which the volunteer commits.
3. Although it contains some routine or clerical duties, it also gives the individual an opportunity to learn new skills and assume increasing responsibility.
4. It is based upon mutual agreement about goals and tasks, often formalized in a written document.
5. A written report or evaluation is the result at the end of the internship.

Because they are prescribed, internships can be immensely more valuable to students than regular volunteer work. They can be listed on resumes and applications just like a paid position, and they provide students with on-the-job skills.

If your local schools at any level lack internships, create your own. A good source to recruit from is children of employees. An internship is one way to keep bored teens occupied. However, there is a word of caution—it is **unacceptable to have one family member supervising another, especially if they are parent and child or older sibling and younger.** To be fair to both parties, placement should be made to a different office.

READ ALOUD

Volunteers who love books, visual arts, and small children can combine their inclinations in read-aloud projects. At the Denver Public Library, the Read Aloud Program is a prescribed effort with certain training, commitment, and actions required. At-risk preschoolers, kids in shelters, and primary grade students receive regular visits during an eight- to ten-week session. Library staff select a variety of appropriate books, and volunteers present them in a distinctive story time that's part of community outreach.

The DPL provides initial training of a two-hour group session. Volunteers agree to read to a selected classroom for eight to ten weeks. This includes preparation for each story time (practice reading), travel, and collecting book packs. Recruitment and training for Read Alouds focuses on several specific times throughout the year, making both activities manageable. Because the individual's commitment in terms of time, location, and length is so specific, many employers are willing to permit their employees to participate even during business hours.

FIGURE 11-4: Former Bronco football star Steve Sewell, now a Denver Bronco Youth Coordinator, reads a story aloud to kids.

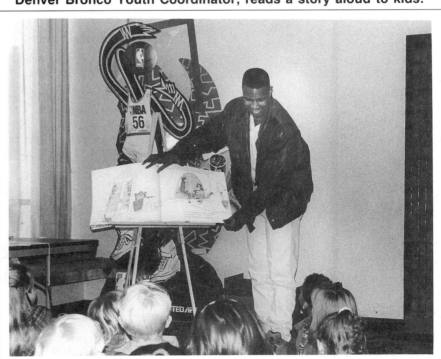

Although the DPL's Read Aloud Program is very structured, the same sequence of activities can be applied to any Read Aloud, in a library or outside it. You'll find that volunteers benefit from training, practice, and a commitment to a particular schedule.

BOARDS AND COMMISSIONS

Another charge for volunteers with particular experience and requirements can be boards and commissions. Because of specialized needs, recruitment is conducted via word of mouth and through personal references.

Prior to beginning recruitment, start by deciding what qualities the board needs. Remember that you are building a unit, not just considering individuals. As with all volunteer positions, a job description is a first step. It is especially important that you give a clear estimate of the amount of time service will demand, number of meetings, and anticipated tasks.

The second step is your library's analysis of its needs. Is the board responsible for fund-raising? Politicking? Receiving and conveying community concerns? Advising on book collections or programs? You will need to obtain board members who can fulfill those functions and feel comfortable doing so.

Appoint a politician to a governing board, right? Remember, most importantly, you're creating a team. Some folks need the spotlight, and you can utilize their skills in various other ways. Often the most successful members of a board are those who are hooked into other networks—for example, the business or education community, political campaigns, civic or service organizations—and they have demonstrated this through their prior activities and professions.

Your next consideration is representation. Agencies increasingly are aware that they need diversity on their boards just as they do in their paid work force and with volunteers. Diversification helps you achieve your goals, because all segments of society represent a library's customer market. No one board can contain each and every ethnic, religious, age, or gender group of the population; but you can actively recruit members to give a better balance.

ADULT LITERACY TUTOR

If your library hosts a literacy program for adults, or wants to do so, you need to recruit people with a unique combination of skills, patience, dedication, and empathy. The Atlanta-Fulton County Library structures its volunteer literacy effort into one-on-one partnerships. No teaching background is required but volunteers receive six hours of training.

Tutoring sessions are scheduled at the mutual convenience of the tutor and the learner at a library with lots of "high-interest/low-vocabulary" reading materials. Computer programs, videodisks, and audio tapes also prove valuable in the multimedia approach to teaching.

You will need to locate one essential component for this program first—experienced leadership, someone (or ones) who is familiar with literacy education efforts and materials, and is able to establish a training program for tutors. Other recruits should agree to establish and maintain a regular schedule of tutoring sessions and exemplify obvious qualities or skills like intelligence and commitment. In addition, you'll be using intuition to screen for intangible qualities such as patience, sensitivity, and determination.

A different challenge is posed by recruitment of adult learners. Whether you engage staff, or volunteers, or a combination of both for this task, you will want to provide them with guidance in responding to inquiries from the public with sensitivity. Literacy programs have garnered tremendous public support thus making them attractive to the business community and service organizations. The Atlanta-Fulton Friends group has partnered with the Junior League of Atlanta and corporations to expand its effort.

HOMEWORK HELP

Another popular volunteer effort provides homework assistance to youngsters. This may be performed over the telephone or in person—neighborhood branches make especially suitable locations. Like the adult literacy program, homework help may require you to purchase some resources and equipment to prepare your library—for example, supplemental and age-targeted resource materials, extra telephone lines, and child-sized chairs and tables. It is also a good idea to establish strong lines of communications with local schools. School personnel can encourage students to avail themselves of assistance. Teachers should convey assignments or at least general areas of study to library staff or key volunteers, preferably before students walk through the library door.

Volunteers work closely with students to verify homework assignments, interpret directions, and teach children to use various resources. They act as liaisons between youngsters and reference librarians and generally supervise the students. These volunteers are not baby-sitters or tutors. They are not to be used as a method for children to avoid learning or to prohibit them from doing their own homework. This is one volunteer position where the goal is to eliminate your job, student by student. As a youngster gains skills and confidence, he or she will become independent in searching out information.

The qualities that make a good homework help volunteer are: being *reliable,* having knowledge of and the ability to use library resources, patience, communication skills with children, and good abilities in reading, writing, and math. Recruits should be willing to make a commitment based on the program's needs either several hours per week for a semester or for one full school year.

Because these volunteers work with a potentially vulnerable population, the library may want to require a criminal records check or prepare written policies on conduct that the recruit must sign.

BOOKSTORE HELP

Many libraries depend on volunteers to plan and implement used book sales. Now as they seek supplemental financial support, the agencies are turning to volunteers to staff permanent library bookstores. They might sell used books year-round, new books, and library-related items such as paper and computer disks, or a combination of both.

If you have been wondering where to place those executive-level recruits, a bookstore may present the ideal opportunity. The purpose of the project is to make money, and individuals with sales, marketing, and accounting skills can help keep you on track. The schedule for these advisory and supervisory functions is flexible enough for you to involve those still employed as well as retirees.

As for the sales staff, look for people who are reliable (that quality seems a universal need), customer-service oriented, with good math skills and an eye for detail. If you hope to utilize volunteers for the entire work schedule, you may want to plan for at least two volunteers at a time to cover unanticipated absences. In addition to agreeing to regular work hours, have your bookstore staff commit to a specific length of time, such as six months or a year.

COSTUMED CHARACTER

Combine acting ability with fun to create a character who personifies the spirit of your library. You'll find that adults react as favorably as children to this character who appears at festivals, fairs, schools, library events, and in the media.

One of the most difficult volunteer positions to fill is a costumed character like the DPL's Bookworm. This character requires the individual to be fearless in the face of the stares of dozens or hundreds of onlookers. He or she also has to possess the sensitivity and sympathy necessary to coax a shy preschooler into handshakes and hugs. However, you don't necessarily need someone with an acting background; the heart of a "ham" is hidden under some very sedate exteriors.

FIGURE 11-5: The DPL Friends Bookworm visits events and fair locations.

As word spreads, you'll get requests for appearances of your character at all hours of the day and night. This is an additional challenge. Ideally, you should have several volunteers you can dress up and schedule as the occasion requires. By recruiting people of different personalities and ages, you can schedule costumed characters who appeal most to preschoolers or adults, on camera or reading stories, whatever suits your situation.

A costumed character can inspire stickers, media appearances, book bags, coloring sheets, and other public relations opportunities. Needless to say, the costume itself should be flexible enough to accommodate volunteers of various sizes. The character can become the symbol of many kinds of family programming.

This overview of programs demonstrates the exciting variety of opportunities available to libraries and volunteers. No matter what their skill level, background, or interest, most people can be accompanied at the most popular and useful of our institutions—the library.

You achieve success when your volunteers fulfill their personal needs while they accomplish tasks that help your library improve its services. The volunteer effort cannot be viewed in isolation, nor can it be expected to produce miracles. Establish goals and objectives for your volunteers that support your other endeavors. Conversely, ensure that your staff and activities confirm the value of volunteerism. You gain not only a dedicated, hardworking group of volunteers but also strong advocates for your institution. The presence of volunteers working alongside of professionals and paid support staff enhances the image of the library as a major community benefit, and a shared volume.

APPENDIX A

TAX DEDUCTIONS FOR VOLUNTEERS

Volunteers cannot deduct the value of volunteer time or services. However, a number of tax benefits are available. In preparing tax returns, volunteers may deduct *unreimbursed out-of-pocket expenses* directly related to their volunteer service *if they itemize deductions.*

Volunteer service must have been contributed to what the Internal Revenue Service terms a "qualifying organization." A general rule is that, when deducting volunteer-related expenses, organizations or companies operated "for-profit" do not qualify. An example of the types of expenditures that volunteers may deduct on their tax returns include:

- bus and cab transportation expenses,
- parking costs and toll fees,
- the cost and expenses of upkeep of special uniforms,
- long-distance telephone bills,
- supplies purchased to perform volunteer duties,
- automobile mileage and expenses for gas and oil,
- dues, fees, or assessments made to a qualified organization, and
- non-cash contributions of property (e.g. clothing, books, household items, equipment, etc.).

Volunteers may deduct automobile expenses at a standard mileage rate established by the IRS or for actual expenses incurred. Volunteers may not deduct general automobile repair and maintenance expenses. Good records for transportation-related costs are a must for volunteers who intend to claim these deductions.

A charitable deduction for travel expenses, including amounts expended for meals and lodging, can be taken only if the travel contains no significant element of personal pleasure, recreation, or vacation.

The "out-of-pocket" requirement eliminates from deduction any amount that is to the direct benefit of the taxpayer, or taxpayer's family, rather than to the organization. If the volunteer receives reimbursement for expenses, he or she may not deduct the expenses.

Keep detailed records that include dates, places, organization, actual amount, and any other pertinent information. New IRS regulations require additional verification for certain types and size of donations, such as a statement from the nonprofit organization. Cash contributions must be an amount actually paid during the taxable year, and not just a pledge. More detailed information can be obtained from the Internal Revenue Service.

This information was obtained from the organization, *Volunteers,* at the National Center, 1991. This organization has now merged into The Points of Light Foundation, 736 Jackson Place, Washington, D.C. 20503.

INDEX